Reading Strands

Understanding Fiction

a
publication
of

National Writing Institute
624 W. University #248
Denton, TX 76201-1889

ISBN 1-888344-16-4

Manufactured in the United States of America

For information, write: National Writing Institute,
                          624 W. University #248
                          Denton, TX 76201-1889

            call: 1 (800) 688-5375
            e-mail: info@writingstrands.com

NATIONAL WRITING INSTITUTE PUBLICATIONS

STUDENTS

Writing Strands Level 1
Writing Strands Level 2
Writing Strands Level 3
Writing Strands Level 4
Writing Strands Level 5
Writing Strands Level 6
Writing Strands Level 7
Writing Exposition
Creating Fiction

Communication and Interpersonal Relationships

Dragonslaying Is For Dreamers

Axel Meets the Blue Men

Axel's Challenge

———

PARENTS/TEACHERS

Evaluating Writing

Reading Strands

Analyzing the Novel:
Dragonslaying Is For Dreamers

ACKNOWLEDGMENTS

I want to express my gratitude to my bright highschool students who taught me how to teach reading.

INTRODUCTION
to the
TEACHERS AND STUDENTS OF READING

This book was written to help you to understand how to discuss fiction with your children. The ideas presented here are based on the knowledge that there can be great joy in reading, and that good literature can enrich anyone's life.

Of course, there is value in solitary reading, but the enjoyment that can be found in stories is greater if it can be shared with others. There are models here of conversations with young readers as a way of showing how reading experiences can be enjoyed by both the young readers and their teachers.

Many adults, faced with the challenge of teaching literature, have the feeling that the job is too great to be reasonable. True, it's a daunting enterprise, but it can be an exciting and fun one. One of the saving aspects of this help you've chosen to give is that there are no "right" answers to the question, "What does this mean?"

Most writers, when asked this question about what they've written, reply, "I don't know, I just wrote it. What's it mean to you?" This is not a bad philosophy to have as a teacher of literature. Most experts agree that the reader must create the "meaning" of what is read. If the work means nothing to the reader, then, for that time and person, the work means nothing.

This is what makes teaching reading so exciting; there are no wrong answers either to that most important question about meaning. How can a child be wrong about what he or she understands? It's possible in factual material to misunderstand authors' intentions, but the reading of fiction doesn't work that way.

The important thing to keep in mind, as you read through this small book, is that reading should be fun. If the young reader doesn't enjoy reading, it may be because reading is seen as work. The reader is either above or below the level of the material, or the material has not been selected with the reader's interests in mind. If your student doesn't like to read, change the program. Forcing a child who doesn't like to read the material may make that child hate the material. Change the material, not the child. The point of this type of reading is the enjoyment of it, not the information it contains.

CONTENTS page

USING *READING STRANDS*
AND THE
PRINCIPLES OF TEACHING LITERATURE

Exchanging information is an activity enjoyed by almost everyone. Think of all the time we spend listening to radio and TV, talking and listening to neighbors and friends, and the tremendous amount of exchange that occurs in our jobs. It's reasonable to think that the better we are at this the more effectively we'll run our lives.

Before we became a people with a written reality who understood the world in terms of printed words, our reality was based on an oral tradition. We understood the world from talking about it. This had its limitations, but it did allow people to communicate face to face and clarify points by asking each other questions. After the invention of the printing press, and until very recently when we began to understand our world electronically, the giver of information and ideas had to speak to a listener/reader from a great distance in this very intimate relationship. The giver of information could no longer speak directly to the listener/reader; there had to be created a "voice," called the narrative voice, which spoke with the black marks (letters) on the page.

Telling a story then became a matter of translation. The reader and this narrative voice had to create the story as they worked together. This may sound strange, for it would seem that words on the page mean very specific things. It's true that the writer, when using the symbols in our alphabet to represent sounds and ideas, has a meaning clearly in mind. This meaning is structured by the experiences and feelings about the concepts presented.

The reader, when interpreting these symbols, brings to the page a unique set of experiences and feelings for the concepts being read about, and can only make sense out of the story in terms of these different conditions. Thus, meaning is created as the translation occurs from black marks to sounds and ideas.

For this reason it's unusual for two people to read a piece of fiction and understand exactly the same things from it. And for the same reason, the author and the reader usually don't understand any piece in the same way. Likewise, there is little assurance that the reader of fiction can know exactly what the writer had in mind when writing. This makes it hard for a teacher to say that an interpretation of a story is wrong or that the reader doesn't understand the piece.

Because all readers of fiction create as they read, what they understand from their reading is, in a very personal way, their reality. Of course the reasonableness of their reading will be structured by their ability to understand the generally accepted meanings of words, and they must have some training to follow the ideas and images presented.

A teacher, in this most complicated process, must have a clear understanding of the general goals in the reading exercise. "What do I want my student to know or experience?"

You, as the teacher, might now think about what you want your student to "get" from the reading you will be doing together. What does your student want? If these goals are similar to yours, you're in luck and your teaching will be easy. Sometimes, when adult and child goals are at odds, reading becomes a chore.

As a teacher/parent you must think about what kind of an adult you would like your student/child to become. It's then your responsibility to give that youngster the experiences which will encourage development along those lines. Reading is one of the important steps children take becoming adults, and the reading they do helps determine the types of people they'll grow into.

You'll find selecting goals that will be compatible with your child's goals easier if you give some organized thought to what you want. Some structure to the process may help you select answers that will please both you and your child.

Of course, there are no wrong selections to these questions. The right goals are what you and your child want and should not be dictated by other people. What you select should be determined by the values held by you, your family, your community and your religion.

For most children, the fun of reading is dependent on its effects on their ways of thinking. If the reader can't relate to the character in a story or to the situation that character is in, or if the reader doesn't care about these things, that reader will not enjoy the narrative. If the young reader can get involved in the lives and situations of the characters, then this experience can be very satisfying.

Reading can become such a rich and rewarding part of life that it's very important that teachers/parents do whatever they can to ensure that their children learn to love it.

To this end I suggest the following:

 1. A beginning reader must have fun reading. It can't be seen as a punishment or as work. The time spent reading each day should be looked forward to with great eagerness, and it's the responsibility of the adults in that child's life to see that this is so.

2. Young readers must observe, as role models, older children, parents and teachers enjoying reading. If the new reader sees this going on, there will be a desire to join in this pleasure.

3. Young readers should see their role models talking about what they're reading. They should see them read bits and pieces to each other from newspapers and magazines. They should see the excitement of this sharing. They'll then want to join in and share with others what they read.

4. Young readers need to have others show an interest in what they're reading and what this makes them think about. It may not be intellectually stimulating for an adult to discuss at length the ideas in a child's see and say book, but watching that young mind develop is one of the most exciting things that can happen to any adult.

5. Young readers need to talk about what they've read. This ensures that they think about the ideas in the stories, that they remember the actions, and that they can feel the excitement of sharing the stories with others. It's when we talk and write about ideas that we really begin to understand them.

6. There are not many other things that a parent/teacher might give to a child that would be more important than a love of books, since they give not just the books but the world of ideas. It makes possible adventures and intellectual challenges found in no other place. It gives the child "rooms" to think in, areas of thought that can be entered in no other way. This child now can have conversations with all of the great minds of history. What a precious thing you've chosen to give.

The materials in this book are not new; they're all available in any good library. I've simply assembled in one volume the most widely used techniques in the comprehension and interpretation of fiction.

I've arranged this material so that homeschooling parents, who have not been trained in this most complicated skill, can teach their children to create meaning from what they've read on their levels of experience.

I recommend that readers choose at least some of their own books. Naturally, guidance may be necessary, but if students are to enjoy reading, then they must be able to read stories of personal interest. Sometimes parents/teachers want their young students to read stories that support academic studies, such as historical fiction. Fine, as long as young students want to read them.

You don't have to read the books your children read to help them understand what they read. You'll ask questions based on your understanding of the techniques described, and your children will answer based on their reading of their stories and books. They'll come to you as experts in what the authors say and you'll meet them as an expert in the techniques. By working together, you and they can determine what the stories mean to them. In this process, they'll learn the techniques of interpretation—which is what you want.

This method of transmitting ideas is helpful in determining how children are understanding the content of their stories. The way students communicate about books gives you insight to their levels of understanding. If their communications leave you confused, you know that your readers need help in organizing their thoughts. When this happens (and it will), don't worry. *Reading Strands* teaches fiction in a way that will help you help your child think, reason, and process information in an organized manner.

This isn't a workbook. It's a resource for teaching literature to children. This means that you'll be using this book much as you'd use a cookbook; not reading it cover to cover, but just that portion you will be immediately using. I've broken the material down into three sections:

1. **Teaching with *Reading Strands*:** Objectives and methods for teaching literature
2. **The Elements of Fiction:** An examination of a story's setting, characters, conflict and resolution and ways to understand each element
3. **Activities:** To promote and reinforce understanding

A suggested plan for discussion of reading:

1. During the week, have your child read a book or story.

2. On Friday have your literature lesson.

Since good reading and good writing work together as model and application, I recommend that you do an exercise in a level of *Writing Strands* and then do a week's work in *Reading Strands*. In this way you'll have a complete language arts program for a year. Each week your children will learn a new technique of effectively transmitting information between readers and writers.

It would be a good idea to teach one item from the "Literary Terms" and one skill or objective from the "Elements of Fiction" section each week. If a child is beginning a new story, begin with a discussion of setting, and progress from there to character discussions and so on. Sometimes you can teach a literary term that coincides with the reading selection, and sometimes not. For example, if your child is reading a mystery, your literary term study could be "what makes a mystery a mystery" as explained in the "Types of Stories" section, and then you could go on and list the actions of a character to study motive, etc. This doesn't have to be the case; you can choose to teach whatever you feel is relevant to your child's understanding at the time.

You won't be teaching your children a body of knowledge about literature. You'll be teaching them how to extract understanding and meaning from any fiction they read so that they'll be able to appreciate literature and benefit from it's values for a lifetime of reading.

Have a good time working with ideas with your children. You both will treasure the experience if you do.

new story - 1st discuss setting
        - 2nd character discussions

4

ESTABLISHING GOALS AND OBJECTIVES

Education is a process which changes the learner. If you accept this concept, then you must expect changes to occur in your child's thinking and/or behavior because of your work together.

Since every relationship of a teacher and a student implies an acceptance of the changes in the student, you must decide what changes are possible and what ones are desirable. In this relationship, both the student and the teacher are responsible for the establishment of goals since both will be so intimately involved in producing results. You, as the teacher, might now think about what you want your student to "get" from the reading you'll be doing together.

What does your student want? Of course, very young children will not be able to articulate these ideas as you will, but still children will "want," and their desires should be taken into consideration. The goals you establish should be written so that they'll be available to you as you work toward them. A year is a long time to remember the goals you've set for your child.

It's easy to establish what is possible for a child; considerable research has been done on this. Two handbooks: *Taxonomy of Educational Objectives: Cognitive Domain* (Bloom, 1984) and the *Taxonomy of Educational Objectives: Effective Domain* (Krathwohl, Bloom, & Masia, 1964) give broad classifications of possible objectives.

It's much harder to establish what is desirable in terms of objectives. These change with each student's attitudes, experiences, values and aspirations for the future. This is a very personal area and there are few guidelines. What is important to think about is that specific objectives are a necessary step in the education of a child. We can't keep a child from growing, but many feel a strong responsibility to direct that growth in specific directions.

There is a difference between goals and objectives in this text. Goals are general statements which have broad interpretation, which you might do well to avoid. The following is a short list of such terms:

1. Grasps the significance of
2. Has an interest in
3. Appreciates
4. Comprehends
5. Thinks critically
6. Understands
7. Learns
8. Respects
9. Enjoys reading

examples of goals — broad scope [handwritten annotation]

5

These directives, along with others such as "Appreciates good books," and "Discusses literature intelligently," are admirable, but are not appropriate for planning lessons. The problem with terms such as these is they don't provide *measurable* interpretive skill. Specific objectives can describe in some detail exactly what cognitive (intellectual) changes you anticipate being the result of the lessons. Compare the list above with the following:

objectives

1. Identify the major forces of conflict in a short story.
2. Describe a character's motivations in a given situation.
3. Recall specific facts - "There were six people on the fifth floor."
4. Anticipate with reasonable accuracy the unread events in a piece of fiction.

One way to avoid the problem of being general is to use verbs (action words) to describe reading objectives. They will then be specific enough that they can be tested. You can tell if your child "recognizes" a word or a plan or a concept or a character or a part of a story plot. It's easy to establish if a youngster can predict what will happen in a story. These terms are usable by both you and your student to determine what changes you expect and which ones you witness having taken place. Some examples of these action verbs are:

1. To recognize
2. To evaluate
3. To predict
4. To volunteer comments
5. To state relationships
6. To list
7. To recall
8. To label actions and motives

As a parent/teacher concerned with instruction, you face the following four jobs:
1. You must **list the goals and objectives** you hope to attain by the end of the learning period (this should include both long term, semester/year and for the entire training period, and short term, unit/week).
2. You must **select the materials** which will allow your students to achieve those goals and objectives (decide which elements of literature you want them to understand).
3. You must help your students **integrate** the learning experiences by producing continuity and sequence (make sure that the materials are connected and that they are progressively more demanding and sophisticated).
4. You must **evaluate progress** being made toward the goals and objectives chosen.

Listing goals and objectives isn't an easy thing to do. The result of not doing it is that there would be experiences for your children, but neither of you would have a clear picture of what changes would be expected to take place as a result of the experiences. An analogy here might help me explain the importance of this pre-teaching activity. If we had millions of dollars and were to decide that we'd go into the car-manufacturing business, we'd face a similar problem. Before we even set up the production lines we'd have to decide what kind of a car we were going to produce. Planning a family sedan is not the same job as planning a two-seat sports car.

The problems of design for performance are much different. We'd have to decide exactly what we were going to make. We'd have to know exactly what each piece was and where it would go and what it would do and what it would look like.

If we didn't do this, we'd have a mess. If every person (experience) were to just toss on a fender or a wheel, and the effort were not coordinated and planned in detail, we might produce a car, if we were lucky, but we wouldn't have confidence in it or have any idea what it would be like.

In that case, all we'd lose is money. But in your case, you have a person you're responsible for. You're in the adult-manufacturing business. Your job is to plan and then make a person, and you'll have to know what you expect this person to be like or you may not be "lucky." To be assured of what this person will turn out to be, you'll have to plan what each piece (experience) will be like and what it will contribute to the "end product" before it's added on.

Following are suggested goals and ideas for helping children in different age groups. These are only suggestions. You may want to develop your own objectives. It's my goal that you become confident teaching literature to the extent that you don't even need to have *Reading Strands* around to have great discussions about books and ideas with your children.

GOALS AND OBJECTIVES
for
VERY YOUNG AND BEGINNING READERS

Some care must be taken in the selection of stories for very young readers and for children who have not yet begun to read. It's not such a bad idea for young children to have their parents select their experiences for them. Many reading experts tell us that children have to develop to an extent before they are able to differentiate between the fantasy of stories and reality. I remember one child who became frightened when a tiger was shown on the television. She was sure that it could jump out of the set and into the living room.

Many fairy stories have characters who might give very young children the impression that witches are real, or that stepmothers are cruel, or that magic is possible, or that some adults who should be trusted might eat children or lock them up. Children have had nightmares for as long as a year after being exposed to some stories. Most people would think this is not such a good thing.

I don't want to be in the position of telling you what to select for your child, but I feel you should think about the following idea. Many stories have a moral lesson or theme. You should think carefully about this when making selections. An example might help you understand what I'm talking about.

I remember a story I read to my son about a little train that had difficulty climbing hills. The larger and older trains encouraged it by chanting to it when it said, "I can't get up, I can't get up." They replied, "Yes, you can. Yes, you can." They encouraged it to say, "I think I can. I think I can." The little train found with positive thinking it could climb the hills just like the older and larger trains. The message here is clear to us, and certainly not lost on little minds: "Think in a positive way and you can do what you want." I'm not saying that this is either good or bad for your child, only that you have to be aware of this and the many other messages in children's stories and decide for yourself.

Some children's books have only middle class families in them which portray very traditional roles for adults. If these role models are what you want for your child, that's fine. Select reading material that supports the values you want to reinforce for your child.

There are books that propose particular viewpoints, just as there are viewpoints expressed in toys. I suggest you examine these viewpoints, value judgements, and stereotypes carefully before you select them for your young child. They may or may not be consistent with the values that are important to your family, as the values expressed by books and toys are not lost on young children.

TEACHING TECHNIQUES

One goal that I'm sure we'd all agree upon when teaching very young or beginning readers, is to lead the learner toward independently being able to construct meaning from the text. To this end you'll want to have strategies when you start to teach your very young reader to understand print. The following listing may help you formulate your own techniques:

I. Prior Knowledge:

A. Before reading to your children, discuss what they already know about the subject. Ask "What do you know about _____?"

B. Ask your readers to list those points they know for sure are true or which could be true, and those they're not certain about. Discuss this list after the reading.

C. Have your readers ask prediction questions before the reading based on what they know about a story. As an example: *"Our reading today is called Bob's New Pet. What kind of a pet do you think it will be?"*

D. Consider prediction questions as you read to them. As for example, *"What do you think will happen next?"*

E. Ask your readers questions after the reading is over. For example: *"What do you think was happening even before this story started?"*

F. Ask your readers questions of comparison between the latest book read and prior books read.

II. Sense Making:

A. Ask your children during the reading, "Does this make sense?"

B. Tell your children to say "Blank" for an unknown word and go on to make sense of the rest of the text.

C. If your children "get stuck" on a word, have them use the beginning consonant sound of the unknown word and the context to make a guess that makes sense and starts with the correct sound.

D. Your children should be as fluent as possible, even if that means skipping unknown words. Fluency, as opposed to choppy, labored reading, leads toward "sense making."

E. Have your children use the pictures on the page as meaning clues.

F. Draw from what your children already know about the situations to help them think about them as they read.

G. During the reading, have your children list in their minds likenesses and differences or compare the subject matter with what they already know about it.

III. **Image Visualization:**

    A. Encourage your children to make a picture or a movie in their minds about the topic or story as you read to them.

    B. Have your children "read" two stories in their minds: one from the words and the other one from the pictures. This is so they can consider similarities and differences.

    C. Have your children stop you if you come to new words they're unfamiliar with.

    D. Encourage your children to draw pictures of what they hear as you read to them, or they can draw after the story is complete.

    E. Use a book that has no words in it and have your children dictate or write the words themselves.

    F. As you read to them, have them "draw" in their minds pictures that would go along with the words, then compare their mental "pictures" with the ones in the book.

    G. Discuss everything you read to them or that they read themselves. Talk about things the authors didn't talk about in the stories, such as the expressions on the faces of the people or what was going on in the next room that the authors didn't let anyone "see" into.

TECHNIQUES WITH EXAMPLES FOR DEVELOPING CRITICAL THINKING SKILLS IN VERY YOUNG AND BEGINNING READERS

The following is a listing of some common techniques for helping young children develop the ability to think and analyze what they hear and read. These labels are ones reading specialists use. You may call them anything you like and feel comfortable with. Whatever they're called, there are good reasons for using them, and they are effective teaching tools.

1. **Recall** - Asking students to tell what just happened in the story. The questions should be specific to a particular event. Recall includes:

   A. **Recall of Details:** Student are asked to locate or identify names of characters, the time the story takes place, the setting, or some incident described in the story.

   B. **Recall of Main Ideas:** Students are asked to identify the main idea of a paragraph or a larger portion of a reading.

   C. **Recall of Sequence:** Students are asked to locate or identify the order of incidents or actions stated in the reading.

   D. **Recall of Comparisons:** Students are asked to locate or identify likenesses and differences among characters, places or events that are compared by the author.

   E. **Recall of Cause and Effect Relationships:** Students are asked to locate or identify reasons for certain incidents, events or actions stated in the reading.

   F. **Recall of Character Traits:** Students are asked to identify or locate statements about characters which help to point out the types of people they are, when such statements were made by the author.

2. **Forecasting** (predicting) - Asking students to tell what will happen next. These questions should be preceded by a short review of the immediate events up to that time. "All the kids come to the party except Janet. What do you think will be the reason why Janet doesn't come?" or, "The bear comes right into the camp and walks into the tent. Do you think that bear will find the food in the box?"

3. **Inferencing** - Asking students to come to conclusions about situations in the story from the information already gained. Inferential comprehension is demonstrated by students when they use a synthesis of the content of a reading, their personal knowledge, intuition and their imaginations as a basis for guessing. Inferencing includes:

A. **Inferring Supporting Details:** Students are asked to guess about additional facts the author might have included in the reading which would have made it more informative, or interesting.

B. **Inferring the Main Idea:** Students are asked to provide the main idea, significance, theme or moral which is not directly stated in the reading.

C. **Inferring Sequence:** Students are asked to guess as to what non-stated action might have taken place between two stated actions or incidents.

D. **Inferring Comparisons:** Students are asked to infer (come to conclusions about) likenesses and differences in characters, times or places. These are centered around ideas such as: then and now, he and she, here and there.

E. **Inferring Cause and Effect Relationships:** Students are asked to guess about the motives of characters and their interactions with others.

F. **Inferring Character Traits:** Students are asked to guess about the nature of characters on the basis of clues presented in the reading.

G. **Predicting Outcomes:** Students are asked to read the start of a selection and then guess the outcome.

4. **Personalizing** - Asking students what they might do in the same situation. This might follow a brief discussion of what the character did. "That girl gives her balloon to that little boy who doesn't have one. I wonder why she does that. If you had been that little girl, would you've given him your balloon? If you were poor and were in a park and saw a rich little girl who had a balloon, would you want her to give you her balloon?"

5. **Character Analysis** - Asking students to talk about the actions of a character and asking them to explain why the character did those things. This is a hard one, and you both will need to practice this. "When it's time for the family to get in the car and follow the moving van out of the driveway and to go to their new house, what does Janet do?" (She hid.) "That's a strange thing to do. That would mean that the family wouldn't be able to go. Why would she do that?" (So they couldn't leave.) "Why doesn't she want to leave?" (She'd miss her friends.) "What does this tell us about how she feels about her friends?"

6. **Discussing Values** - If you want to deal with values with your children, this is a good technique for doing so. Stories give an excellent opportunity to bring up various values and how they affect our decisions and govern our lives. "When Bob tells John that he'd taken the candy from the store and hadn't paid for it, John has a problem, didn't he?" (He sure did.) "What are the three things he can do?" (He could tell on Bob or he could try and talk Bob into giving the candy back or paying for it or he could forget it.) "What do you think would be the moral, Christian, kind, legal, responsible, proper, necessary, important, or practical thing for John to do?" (suggesting an action dependent upon your value system.)

7. **Examining the Resolution** (ending) - Asking students to talk about the ending of the story. This gives them the idea that stories might end in lots of different ways and still be good stories. It stimulates children to think creatively about what has been read. "What do you think about Anne's father stringing fencing around the garden?" (He wanted to keep out the rabbits so they wouldn't eat all of the plants.) "What is the purpose of the garden?" (To please Anne. She couldn't go outside because she was in a wheelchair. She wanted to sit in the window and look at the garden growing.) "Do you like that ending?" (No, I feel sad for the rabbits, and so does Anne.) "Why?" (Because she liked to watch the rabbits eating in the garden.) "Would you like the story to end with the rabbits eating the garden and Anne watching them do it?" (Yes.) "Would you like Anne's father better if he just plants more flowers for the rabbits to eat?"

There is additional help for teaching meaning to young readers on page 66 and stories and example dialogues on page 76.

13

TEACHING CRITICAL THINKING

This story is followed by a tape recorded discussion between a five-year-old girl and a reading expert and demonstrates how young children can be taught to think critically while being read to.

THE WELL-WORN PATH

It was the first warm day of spring. The birds were singing. There were rabbits eating grass beside the railroad tracks. There was even a turtle crossing the dirt road down in the big field by the pond. As far as you could see the railroad track stretched straight away in both directions.

Near the pond was an old water wheel where the miller used to grind grain to make flour. The building was empty and the tracks that led away from the main tracks to it were covered with weeds and tall grasses.

It so happened that on this day the smallest train was making its first run. A run is when it goes from one place to another place.

This was an exciting day! The first time out alone. You might not think that trains can feel good about things, but that is not true. They can. And this one did. This smallest train was so happy to be out and on its first run.

It had been given oil. It had been fed lots of fuel to make it go. It had been polished until its sides were shiny. If you had been standing next to the small engine, you would have been able to see yourself, as in a mirror, in almost any part of it.

The station master gave his orders. The smallest train was to go straight to Hooterville, the next train town. It was not to stop. It was not to turn off on any of the side tracks. It was not do anything but stay on the straight path to Hooterville.

The station master turned the lights at the side of the track from red to green. Green means that it could start. He waved his lantern. It was time to go! Oh boy, time to go. Off to Hooterville. All alone!

The smallest train started to move. Very slowly its wheels began to turn. Careful. . . Careful. . .Start slow. Don't start fast. Take it easy. Watch what you're doing. Don't get frisky. Not too fast—too fast—too fast.

The air was warm. The sky was blue. The birds were up. The track was clear. The smallest train could hear the wheels singing on the track. This is fun. This is fun. This is fun. It was going, going, going.

Up ahead there was a pond. It was blue and there were ducks. There was a waterwheel near the pond. There was a track off the main track that curved down to the pond. This looks interesting. Let's take a look. Take a look. Take a look. Let's look. Let's look. Let's look.

The smallest train turned off the main track and glided down to the pond. It watched the ducks. It looked at the waterwheel. It saw the rabbits eating grass by the tracks.

But there was the end of the track! There was no more track! The smallest train stopped. Now what?. . .Now what?. . .Now what?

There was nowhere to go. It couldn't go ahead. It couldn't go to the right. It couldn't go to the left. It was stuck! What would the station master say? "On the first run the smallest train gets stuck." How embarrassing. It tried very hard to think of what to do.

Up! If it couldn't go right, and couldn't go left, and couldn't go ahead, all that was left was up. It must try and go up. All it had to do was learn to fly, and then it could go back to the main track.

The smallest train saw a movement over by the pond. The ducks! They knew how to fly. The smallest train watched the ducks flying over the pond. It studied how they moved their wings. How they held their tails. How they took off from the water.

Finally the smallest train was ready to fly. It knew how it was done. It strained and lifted until it could hear its metal stretch and creak. It flapped the loose plates along its sides. The doors on the cars opened and then banged shut. Smoke roared from its little funnel. Its wheels clattered against the rails. If desire could produce results, the smallest train would have lifted off of the tracks and flown, but it could not fly. The cars of the smallest train settled back to the tracks. The engine relaxed and wheezed back down with a groaning that made the rabbits look up. The effort had made the smallest train so tired that it could hardly keep its lights on.

What now?. . .What now?. . .What now?

Stuck at the side of the pond with the ducks and the rabbits and the waterwheel. And the turtle! Even the turtle could cross the tracks.

"This is very sad. Even a turtle can do it, and I can't," the smallest train said right out loud. "I will have to wait until help comes."

And wait it did. All the rest of the morning the smallest train sat there by the waterwheel all alone. When the sun was right overhead, and it was noon, the smallest train knew that the other trains were getting oil and fuel for lunch. But there was none for the smallest train.

It sat there alone for the afternoon. It could hear other trains in the distance but could see none of them. Crickets began to hop on its wheels. A family of mice moved in under one of the cars.

The smallest train began to think that there would be no other trains on the track to Hooterville that day at all. "I might have to spend the night here all alone," thought the smallest train.

But other trains did come! Big trains roared by. The ground shook. The air filled with smoke. The ducks dove to the bottom of the pond. The rabbits hid in their holes. The turtle pulled in its neck and hid in its shell. The smallest train blew its whistle and called to the big trains as they raced past. Heeelp!. . .Heeelp!. . .Heeelp!

The big trains could not hear the smallest train. They were in a hurry to get to Hooterville! They didn't have time to look for a small lost train.

Just before the sun set one of the big trains saw or heard the smallest train. We will never know which it was, but it was just in time. The smallest train was so tired it almost couldn't hoot any more. Water dripped from its small front lights. Oil ran from its sides. The last of its fuel gurgled in hungry tanks.

Its lights were dim now, and oil was staining its sides. If you had been standing right next to the smallest train, you wouldn't have been able to see yourself in any part of it.

The big train stopped in a cloud of steam and said, "Back up. . .Back up. . .Back up. Back to the straight main track." The smallest train tried as hard as it could to back up, but it was such a job, and it was sooo tired.

The big train said, "Back up! Back up! Back up! Back to the main track. You can do it. You can do it. You can do it." The smallest train straaained and could move just a bit. Just a bit more. A bit more. More. More. Then some more. Now it was backing up. Backing up. Up. It was back to the main track!

The big train said, "Follow me on the straight track. I'll lead. You follow. I'll lead, you follow. You follow, You follow. You follow."

The smallest train found it easy on the straight track. It kept up with the big train. On they flew to Hooterville. The big train in front. The smallest train behind. Together they flew. To Hooterville. It was easy. It was fun. It was great! The main, straight track—the only way to go. Hooterville, Hooterville, heere. . . weee. . . come!

In the reading and conversation which follows, notice the use of the above seven techniques for developing critical thinking in young children and how they were used by this teacher.

THE WELL-WORN PATH

It was the first warm day of spring. The birds were singing. There were rabbits eating grass beside the railroad tracks. There was even a turtle crossing the dirt road down in the big field by the pond. As far as you could see, the railroad track stretched straight away in both directions.

Teacher: What kind of a day do you think it was?
Child: A nice day.
Teacher: How do you know that?
Child: It was warm. And it was spring.
Teacher: Good. But what if the people in a story want to go ice skating? Then what would the day have to be to be nice?
Child: Then it would have to be cold.
Teacher: Yes, because the ice would melt, wouldn't it?
Child: Yes.
Teacher: Then is a nice day cold or warm?
Child: (After a pause) It depends on what the people want to do.
Teacher: Sure it would. Good for you. Now, where was this. In town?
Child: No, in the country, 'cause there was rabbits and turtles.
Teacher: Yes, there were.

Near the pond was a waterwheel where the miller used to grind grain to make flour.

Teacher: Do you know what a waterwheel is?
Child: No.

Teacher: It's a great big wheel that turns when it's put in a stream of water. It's hooked up to another wheel made of stone that is used to grind up seeds to make the kind of flour we use to make cakes and bread.

The building was empty, and the tracks that led away from the main tracks to it were covered with weeds and tall grasses.

Teacher: What does that make you think of when the story says that there were weeds and tall grasses growing in the train tracks?
Child: Nobody lived there.
Teacher: All right. If anybody got in there it would be lonely, wouldn't it?
Child: Yes.

It so happened that on this day the smallest train was making its first run. A run is when it goes from one place to another place.

This was an exciting day! The first time out alone. You might not think that trains can feel good about things, but that is not true. They can. And this one did. This smallest train was so happy to be out and on its first run.

Teacher: Do you think trains can feel things?
Child: Yes.
Teacher: How would you feel if you were going to go somewhere alone for the very first time?
Child: Excited and glad.

It had been given oil. It had been fed lots of fuel to make it go. It had been polished until its sides were shiny. If you had been standing next to the small engine, you would have been able to see yourself, as in a mirror, in almost any part of it.

Teacher: That must have been a pretty train. Do you know what fuel is?
Child: Yes, its like gas for the car.
Teacher: Good for you.

The station master gave his orders.

Teacher: The station master would be the smallest train's boss wouldn't he?
Child: Yes.

The smallest train was to go straight to Hooterville, the next train town. It was not to stop. It was not to turn off on any of the side tracks. It was not to do anything but stay on the straight path to Hooterville.

Teacher: What do you think? Will the train stay on the straight track, or will it go off on some other track?
Child: It will stay on the straight track.

17

Teacher: Okay, we'll see here what happens.

The station master turned the lights at the side of the track from red to green. Green means that it could start. He waved his lantern. It was time to go! Oh boy, time to go. Off to Hooterville. All alone!

Teacher: Listen to the rhythm here of the train. You'll almost be able to hear the train talking.

The smallest train started to move. Very slowly its wheels began to turn. Careful. . . Careful. . . Start slow. Don't start fast. Take it easy. Watch what you're doing. Don't get frisky. Not too fast—too fast—too fast.

Teacher: Can you hear the wheels talking with the rhythm of the sentences?
Child: Yes.

The air was warm. The sky was blue. The birds were up. The track was clear. The smallest train could hear the wheels singing on the track. This is fun. This is fun. This is fun. It was going, going, going.

Teacher: Hear it again, there?
Child: I hear it.

Up ahead there was a pond.

Teacher: What would you expect to find on a pond?
Child: A duck.
Teacher: Let's read on and see if you're right or not.

It was blue and there were ducks. There was a waterwheel near the pond. There was a track off the main track that curved down to the pond. This looks interesting. Let's take a look. Take a look. Take a look. Let's look. Let's look. Let's look.

The smallest train turned off the main track and glided down to the pond. It watched the ducks. It looked at the waterwheel. It saw the rabbits eating grass by the tracks.
But there was the end of the track! There was no more track! The smallest train stopped.

Teacher: What happened to the tracks?
Child: It stopped.
Teacher: What do you mean, it stopped?
Child: That was the end of the tracks. There weren't any more.

Now what?. . .Now what?. . .Now what?

Teacher: *What can the train do now? What would you do if you were a train and you ran out*
of tracks to run on.
Child: *I'd back up to the straight track.*
Teacher: *Why?*
Child: *So I could go.*
Teacher: *Good for you. Let's see what the smallest train does.*

There was nowhere to go. It couldn't go ahead. It couldn't go to the right. It couldn't go to the left. It was stuck! What would the station master say? "On the first run the smallest train gets stuck." How embarrassing. It tried very hard to think of what to do.

Up! If it couldn't go right, and couldn't go left, and couldn't go ahead, all that was left was up. It must try and go up. All it had to do was learn to fly, and then it could go back to the main track.

Teacher: *Can trains fly?*
Child: *No!*
Teacher: *Why not?*
Child: *(after a short pause) They don't have any wings.*
Teacher: *Do you think that this smallest train knows this?*
Child: *What?*
Teacher: *Would a train know that it didn't have any wings?*
Child: *I don't know.*
Teacher: *Let's see what happens.*

The smallest train saw a movement over by the pond. The ducks! They knew how to fly. The smallest train watched the ducks flying over the pond. It studied how they moved their wings. How they held their tails. How they took off from the water.

Finally the smallest train was ready to fly. It knew how it was done.

Teacher: *Does this train think it will be able to fly?*
Child: *Yes.*
Teacher: *How did it learn to fly?*
Child: *By watching the ducks.*
Teacher: *Is that going to work?*
Child: *No. Trains can't fly.*

It strained and lifted until it could hear its metal stretch and creak. Its bell rang and rang and rang. It flapped the loose plates along its sides. The doors on the cars opened and then banged shut. Smoke roared from its little funnel. Its wheels clattered against the rails. If desire could produce results,. . .

Teacher: *What does that mean?*
Child: *What?*
Teacher: *"If desire could produce results."*

Child: I don't know.
Teacher: Okay, we'll talk about that after we finish the story, because I want to find out what happens, don't you?
Child: Yeah.

. . .the smallest train would have lifted off of the tracks and flown, but it could not fly. The cars of the smallest train settled back to the tracks. The engine relaxed and wheezed back down with a groaning that made the rabbits look up. The effort had made the smallest train so tired that it could hardly keep its lights on.
    What now?. . .What now?. . .What now?

Teacher: Why was the train so tired?
Child: It tried to fly.
Teacher: Good. And it wore itself out, didn't it?
Child: Yes.

Stuck at the side of the pond with the ducks and the rabbits and the waterwheel. And the turtle! Even the turtle could cross the tracks. "This is very sad. Even a turtle can do it and I can't," the smallest train said right out loud. "I will have to wait until help comes."

Teacher: What does that make you feel like?
Child: Sad.
Teacher: You feel like the train feels?
Child: Yes.
Teacher: If we tried to fly really hard, do you think it would work for us. Could we fly?
Child: No. We don't have wings.
Teacher: It takes wings?
Child: Yes.
Teacher: But what about frogs?
Child: Frogs can't fly!
Teacher: Oh, yes, I forgot. Let's see what happens here.

And wait it did. All the rest of the morning the smallest train sat there by the waterwheel all alone. When the sun was right overhead, and it was noon,. . .

Teacher: What happens at noon?
Child: We eat lunch.
Teacher: Do you think the train is hungry?
Child: Trains don't eat.
Teacher: Maybe this is a special train in this story. Let's find out.

. . .the smallest train knew that the other trains were getting oil and fuel for lunch. But there was none for the smallest train.

It sat there alone for the afternoon. It could hear other trains in the distance but could see none of them. Crickets began to hop on its wheels. A family of mice moved in under one of the cars.

Teacher: *That's a nice place for the mice to make a house. Right under the train. What do you think of that?*
Child: *What if the train moves?*
Teacher: *Where can it go? It can't go to the right. It can't go to the left. It learned it can't go up. There is no other place for it to go.*
Child: *Backward!*
Teacher: *Backward? Can trains go backward?*
Child: *Sure they can. The smallest train could back up.*
Teacher: *Is that what you would do?*
Child: *Yes.*
Teacher: *What do you think will happen here? Will the smallest train back up?*
Child: *I don't know.*
Teacher: *Let's find out.*

The smallest train began to think that there would be no other trains on the track to Hooterville that day at all. "I might have to spend the night here all alone," thought the smallest train.

Teacher: *I didn't know trains get lonely.*
Child: *I didn't either.*
Teacher: *That's kind of sad to think of the smallest train all alone for maybe the whole night.*
Child: *I know.*

But other trains did come! Big trains roared by. The ground shook. The air filled with smoke. The ducks dove to the bottom of the pond. The rabbits hid in their holes. The turtle pulled in its neck and hid in its shell. The smallest train blew its whistle and called to the big trains as they raced past. Heeelp!. . .Heeelp!. . .Heeelp!

The big trains could not hear the smallest train. They were in a hurry to get to Hooterville! They didn't have time to look for a small lost train.

Just before the sun set, one of the big trains saw or heard the smallest train. We will never know which it was, but it was just in time. The smallest train was so tired it almost couldn't hoot any more. Water dripped from its small front lights. Oil ran from its sides. The last of its fuel gurgled in hungry tanks.

Its lights were dim now, and oil was staining its sides. If you had been standing right next to the smallest train you wouldn't have been able to see yourself in any part of it.

Teacher: *Remember in the beginning of the story that the train was so shiny that you could have seen yourself in any part of it?*
Child: *Yes.*

Teacher: Why couldn't you see yourself now?
Child: Because it had oil all over it. It was dirty.
Teacher: Good.

The big train stopped in a cloud of steam and said, "Back up. . .Back up. . .Back up. Back to the straight, main track." The smallest train tried as hard as it could to back up, but it was such a job, and it was sooo tired.

The big train said, "Back up! Back up! Back up! Back to the main track. You can do it. You can do it. You can do it."

Teacher: What was the big train trying to do for the smallest train?
Child: Trying get it to back up.
Teacher: It was giving it encouragement. It was saying, "You can do it."

The smallest train straaained and could move just a bit. Just a bit more. A bit more. More. More. Then some more. Now it was backing up. Backing up. Up. It was back to the main track!

The big train said, "Follow me on the straight track." I'll lead. You follow. I'll lead, you follow. You follow, You follow. You follow."

The smallest train found it easy on the straight track. It kept up with the big train. On they flew to Hooterville. The big train in front. The smallest train behind. Together they flew. To Hooterville. It was easy. It was fun. It was great! The main, straight track—the only way to go. Hooterville, Hooterville, heere. . . weee. . . come!

Teacher: Was that a happy story?
Child: Yes.
Teacher: But the smallest train couldn't fly.
Child: I know.
Teacher: Did the smallest train get what it wanted?
Child: What did it want?
Teacher: What do you think it wanted?
Child: To get to Hooterville?
Teacher: Good for you. Let's read another story tomorrow.
Child: Let's read another one now. It's not too late.
Teacher: You want to read another story?
Child: Yes.
Teacher: That is what you desire?
Child: What does that mean?
Teacher: Desire?
Child: Yes.
Teacher: It means that is what you want. Desire is want.
Child: That's what I desire then.
Teacher: Does what you desire always happen?
Child: No.

B. **Identification with Characters:** The student is asked to identify the literary techniques which prompt sympathy or empathy, and what the author has done to make the reader feel like, or want to be like a character, or not to feel for a character and the position that character is in.

C. **Reactions to Language:** The student is asked to respond to the author's choice of words in terms of denotation (specific meaning) and connotation (the suggested association or implication) and the influence they have on the intended reader's emotions and thinking. This could include examination of similes and metaphors and their effects.

D. **Imagery:** The student is asked to recognize the author's ability to create "pictures" with words, and to identify what the author has done to engage the reader's sensory imagination.

Make sure you read the stories and example dialogues starting on page 76.

Teacher: Then we don't get things just because we want them?
Child: No.
Teacher: Then desire doesn't produce results.
Child: No.
Teacher: That was in the story. Remember? The story said, "If desire could produce results. . .," and I said that we'd talk about that after we'd read the story?
Child: Yes.
Teacher: We just talked about it. Do you know now what that means, "If desire could produce results?"
Child: It means I can't have another story just because I want one?
Teacher: Right!

GOALS AND OBJECTIVES
for
READERS AGED SEVEN AND ABOVE

I. **Literal Recognition or Recall:** Literal comprehension begins with the recall of ideas, information and events in the material read. This would include the recall of:

 A. **Details:** To locate or identify names of characters, the time the story takes place, or the setting
 B. **Main Ideas:** To identify the main idea of a paragraph or a larger portion of reading
 C. **Sequence**: To locate or identify the order of incidents or actions
 D. **Comparisons:** To locate or identify likenesses and differences among characters, places, or events
 E. **Cause and Effect Relationships:** To locate or identify reasons for certain incidents, events or actions
 F. **Character Traits:** To identify or locate statements about characters which indicate the types of people they are

II. **Inference:** Inferential comprehension is demonstrated by the students when they use a synthesis of the content of a reading, their personal knowledge, intuition and their imaginations as a basis for guessing. Have your readers infer (come to conclusions about) the following:

 A. **Supporting Details:** To guess about conditions or situations which the author didn't include
 B. **The Main Idea:** To provide the main idea, significance, theme or moral which is not directly stated in the reading
 C. **Sequence:** To guess what non-stated action might have taken place between two stated actions or incidents or what might have happened before a story begins
 D. **Comparisons:** To recognize likenesses and differences in characters, times or places which are centered around ideas such as: then and now, here and there or two characters
 E. **Cause and Effect Relationships:** To guess about actions and the resulting consequences
 F. **Character Motives:** To understand the motives of characters based on actions and their interactions with others, and to determine if they are produced by internal or external forces
 G. **Character Traits:** To guess about the nature of characters based on clues presented in the reading

WORKING WITH READERS
IN
GRADES SEVEN AND ABOVE

Your older children will come to their reading with a good bit of understanding about how the world works and how they should and can deal with it. You'll find that they will react to what they read much differently now than they did when they were young. They'll come to conclusions that you might not understand or agree with, and you must keep in mind that they are comprehending what they read based on the experiences that they've had and not on the ones that you tell them about.

As you work together, you should come to expect and appreciate the differences in how you both understand fiction. Accept these differences and encourage your children to explore their minds as they read.

Below are some guidelines for your work with them. You might create your own processes of judging how your children appreciate their experiences.

I. **Evaluation:** Evaluation is demonstrated by students when they make judgments about the content of a reading by comparing it with external criteria (references outside the story) such as information supplied by the parents, authorities on the subject or by personal experience. These might include worth, suitability, truthfulness, quality or reasonableness. Evaluation includes:

 A. **Judgments of Reality or Fantasy:** Your students are asked to determine whether events or characters could have existed within the context of the narrative.
 B. **Judgements of Fact:** Your students are asked to decide whether the author has given information which can be supported with facts in the text.
 C. **Judgements of Worth or Acceptability:** Your students are asked to pass judgments on a character's actions. Was the character right or wrong, or good or bad based on the character's situation and experience?

II. **Appreciation:** Appreciation has to do with students responding to forms, styles and structures employed by authors to stimulate desired reactions in the readers. This has to do with the students' appreciation of the plots, themes, settings, incidents, and characters and the selection of language. Appreciation includes:

 A. **Emotional Response:** The student is asked to determine what the author has done to stimulate emotional reactions such as cheerfulness, happiness, love, hate, fear, tenderness, sentimentality, excitement, suspense, curiosity, boredom or sadness.

THE SOCRATIC METHOD
OF TEACHING TO ALL AGES

Readers, and in particular young readers, need to talk about what they've read. This ensures that they think about the ideas in the stories, that they remember the actions, and that they can feel the excitement of sharing the stories with others. It's when we talk and write about ideas that we really begin to understand them.

One technique used in education is the Socratic Method. Named for Socrates, the Greek philosopher, this method advocates teaching a student *how* to think, not *what* to think, and creates understanding in an easy, conversational way.

There is no set of guidelines for teaching with the Socratic method, but there are elements that characterize it. The discussions:

- Begin with the teacher having a specific objective in mind
- Are open-ended.
- Are informal.
- Are not a testing of the student.
- Are conversations between teacher and student in which the teacher leads the student to an understanding of a concept. In this case, each conversation is centered on one of the methods of understanding a story.
- Are characterized by a person who understands the significance of an experience another has, and helps that person to understand it by asking questions designed to lead that person's thinking in the direction that will produce a like understanding. The best way for you to understand this process is to read Plato's *Republic* in which Socrates has conversations using this method. Or, you could look at the conversations in this book as examples of this process. If you do, you'll notice that there are questions similar the ones below:

"Do you think. . .?"
"Can you see how. . .?"
"What happened to. . .?"
"What can they do now?"
"What do you think?"
"Why was it that way?"
"What caused that?"
"If that's true, doesn't that lead to. . .?"
"What's the next logical step in that type of thinking?"
"Don't you feel that. . .?"
"Now that you've seen that, isn't the next conclusion this. . .?"
"What you've just said doesn't seem to be consistent with what you said a moment ago."
"What's the difference between the two situations?"

In addition to asking questions, these dialogues give the teacher a chance to clarify points the students are unfamiliar with, i.e., difficult concepts, words, periods of history, etc. There remains one question a teacher must consider before beginning a Socratic discussion: "How do I evaluate the outcome of these sessions?"

Experience and Meaning

It used to be that teachers of literature told their students what the authors' themes were and what they meant. Now we know enough about reading to know that reading is a very creative process. All authors can do is leave marks on a piece of paper. It's true that they have an understanding of what those marks mean, but they're no longer there when a reader picks up the work. Those black marks represent letters in our alphabet. Each letter represents a sound. Those sounds in combination represent words. Words represent objects and ideas. This complicated system of representation means that there must be a good deal of interpretation on the part of the reader.

For this reason it's unusual for two people to read the same story and understand exactly the same things from it. And for the same reason, the author and the reader usually don't understand any piece in exactly the same way, because an author also draws from his own experience in telling a story. For example, authors from periods prior to the twentieth century are often concerned about health issues, and those issues are reflected in their writing. A person reading such material wouldn't fully relate to the seriousness of described health difficulties (conflicts), and much of what the author intended to communicate would be lost. Factors such as these make it hard for a teacher to say that an interpretation of a story is wrong or that the reader doesn't understand the piece.

A reader must make meaning from what is read on the basis of the experiences that that person has had. For instance, I've had a lot of experience with war. My son, also, has dealt with our country being at war, but his experience is much different from my own. If he and I were to read the same story and it had the word *war* in it, he and I would be reading different words because we'd interpret those black marks that make the word *war,* based on our different experiences.

If you were to come across the word *war* in a book or story and you were thirty-five to forty-five years old, it would have particular significance to you, for you would have been a young person during the war with Vietnam. You would have been torn at that time by your feelings of patriotism and your disgust of the killing. If your ten-year-old child were to come across the word in the same story, there would be none of those associations, and the word would have to be understood from what the child had heard about the experience. If the child were six or seven years old, there could be very little understanding of the word. If your grandparents were to read the story to or with the child, their understanding would have to be influenced by their living through and possibly fighting in the Korean War or in the Second World War. Thus, they'd have very strong feelings about the word that the child would have no access to.

The only answers then, which can be right or wrong, are answers to specific questions about a story, such as recall of names or sequence of events. Answers to non-factual, non-specific types of questions will be based on the readers' experiences with the concepts discussed, and based on their reality, and will reflect the values held by you, your family, your religion, and your community. Your children's understanding has to be different from yours, too. Eventually, they'll see fiction closer to the way you do, but only after they have had many of the same experiences that you've had.

ELEMENTS OF FICTION
and
WAYS TO UNDERSTAND THEM

Fiction can be interpreted through an understanding of each of the elements listed below. A thorough examination follows which will help your child derive meaning from any fiction.

I. Setting
 A. Time
 B. Place

II. Characters
 A. Actions
 B. Motives for acting as they do
 C. Relationships and how these affect their actions
 D. Speech
 E. Personality, or, the kinds of people they are (stingy, thoughtful, etc.) and how this affects their lives
 F. Weaknesses and strengths and what effect these have on how they function
 G. Physical characteristics and how these affect their behavior
 H. Intelligence and/or schooling and how these characteristics affect them in their relationships

III. Conflict
 The problem of the story (the situation the characters face). Usually this takes the form of:
 A. Person against Person
 B. Person against Nature
 C. Person against Society
 D. Person against Self

IV. Resolution
 The resolving of all the conflicts, both the main and those in any sub-plots.
 A. The establishing of what happens to the characters after the conflicts are resolved
 B. There might be an explanation of how the "problem" was understood and resolved. This is common in mystery stories and novels.

V. Point of view
 A. Person
 B. Tense
 C. Attitude
 D. Involvement
 E. Knowledge
 F. Perspective

I. SETTING

The setting of a story consists of the *time* and the *place* in which a story occurs. *Time* includes season, or time of day, and *place* defines the location of the action. The initial setting is usually described in the first chapter because the factors involved in it help define the characters and conflict. It's not uncommon for the setting to change as characters face new experiences and changing circumstances. The establishment of the setting for stories or novels or for scenes in them are a major factor in creating the mood of the pieces. Mood in fiction is established by controlling the description of the following factors:

1. Setting
    A. Colors and patterns
    B. The orientation and size of structures
    C. Lights and shadows
2. Characters' attitudes toward place, situation, and other characters
3. Prior events
4. Sentence length and variety
5. Word choice
6. Movement
7. Dialogue
8. Narrator attitude

A. UNDERSTANDING THE SETTING

1. **By Time**

    a. **Clothing style:** Young readers can roughly determine a time period by clothing style, i.e., if the story takes place in "olden times" or in more modern times.

    b. **Clothing type:** Indicates whether the characters live in the city or country, if they have money or are poor, how old they are, and whether they come from families which place importance on style or utility.

    c. **Dialogue/Language:** Reflects time periods by language styles, such as Shakespeare's use of "thee" and "thou."

    d. **Machines, for type and period:** Descriptions/illustrations of machines and modes of transportation are good indicators of time. Even very young children can get a feeling for the time of the story if horses are pictured pulling wagons or carriages. Modern cars, farm machines and airplanes are good clues. Weapons also give good indications, i.e., guns, bows, swords, and clubs.

    e. **Objects in the backgrounds of pictures:** These often give information about time periods. Houses and commercial buildings can, by their architecture, indicate periods.

2. **By Place**

   a. **The topography or geology:** The way the neighborhood is contoured or the part of the country in which the story takes place (the location of the action) If a picture shows deciduous trees (those that lose their leaves each year), that indicates the action takes place in the northern part of the world. If the trees shown are palms or the plants are those that grow in areas that are warm all year, then the young reader will know that the action takes place in semitropical regions. In either case, the attitudes and actions of the characters would be influenced by the geography.

   b. **The immediate setting:** Details concerning the lifestyles of the characters. If the story occurs on a farm, there would be differences in the children's lifestyles such as doing chores and getting up early, compared to lifestyles of children growing up in the city.

   c. **Character attitudes:** If the action takes place downtown in stores, the adults would have different attitudes toward children who they might or might not know, than would the children's parents or other neighborhood adults.

EXAMPLE OF SOCRATIC
DIALOGUE REGARDING SETTING

An understanding of the setting of a piece of fiction will help a reader understand elements such as character motivation, the mood of the times, character action, and the political, economic, religious and social conditions of the period. Of course, you can only deal with one or two aspects of setting at a time. But then, you've got years to work with your children. The example below is one of teaching setting as the background to the action in the story.

Teacher:	*There was lots of action in that story, wasn't there? Did you like it?*
Reader:	*I sure did. But some of it was sad to read.*
Teacher:	*Like what part?*
Reader:	*When the big house burns and all the people are standing in the yard watching all their possessions destroyed.*
Teacher:	*It might help you to understand the feelings on both sides of the war if you knew something about what their lives were like before the war and what the war was all about.*
Reader:	*I don't know anything about that.*
Teacher:	*If all you understood was that some soldiers came and burned the house and barns and butchered all the stock and turned all the slaves free, then you wouldn't really understand all that there is to this story.*
Reader:	*Tell me about that.*

Teacher: *In the South, before the war, much of the economy was based on slavery. Big plantations required a lot of work. They needed many people to work the fields because there weren't tractors and farm machines then like there are now. Their whole lives were based on having cheap labor. So, slavery was a way of life for many of the land owning white families of the South.*

Reader: *Why did the soldiers come and burn the farm?*

Teacher: *The North was trying to hold the country together, and the South thought they would have better lives if they started their own country. So, the war was about whether we'd have one or two countries here in America. The North had invaded the state where this story takes place and they were destroying the ability of the South to produce cotton and food for the southern army. The soldiers were freeing the slaves, and in that process they were destroying the lives of the southern farmers.*

Reader: *Who was right?*

Teacher: *Let's look at all the things in the story the author has the narrative voice show us, and that'll give us some ways to think about right and wrong. Okay?*

II. CHARACTERS

The characters are the people in the story. In children's books, the characters are sometimes animals, aliens, or anything else that can take on a personality. In order for a reader to understand a story, the characters must be understood. For most children, the fun of reading depends on this understanding. If the reader can't relate to a character or to the situation that character is in, or if the reader doesn't care about these things, that reader will not enjoy the narrative. But when the reader becomes involved in the lives and situations of the characters, then this experience will be very satisfying.

When an author writes, there is the entire world that may be described. Of course, this would not make sense and would take forever, so an author has to select that which is important to the story and choose not to describe what's not as important. This is true of characters. By taking note of what the author has chosen to describe, a reader can concentrate on what the author feels is significant. If a character is presented in detail, then the author must want the reader to concentrate on that particular one. The things described may also be clues to something that will happen later in the story.

Everything an author writes about characters is designed to create a reaction in the reader to those characters. This often produces a reaction called **character identification** and is carefully orchestrated by an author so that readers can empathize with the predicaments and joys the characters experience. There are three methods a writer uses in this character identification process:

1. Creating a character who is very **similar** to the intended readership (audience) so that the readers will recognize that they are like the character
2. Creating a character who the intended readership would **like to be like**
3. Creating a character who the readers **know so much about** that they *understand* why the character acts and reacts as he or she does

A. UNDERSTANDING CHARACTERS: A reader can gain an understanding of characters by examining:

1. **The roles they play in the story:** There are two types of roles for main characters in a story: the *protagonist* and the *antagonist*. These terms represent the characters or forces. The conflict of a story results from the struggle between these opposing forces.

   a. **Protagonist:** This character or force is the main character that wants something. The Latin prefix **pro** means to advance, **agonistes** is the word for actor or contestant. Young readers might identify him as the "good guy."

   b. **Antagonist:** The character or force opposing the protagonist; the "bad guy." This is remembered because the word starts with **ant,** a variation of *anti*, the prefix meaning *against*. This is usually the side of the conflict with the bad guy or the bad force, like a "big bad wolf," or harsh weather or greed.

2. **Their personality characteristics:** An understanding of a character will occur when your reader examines its personality using the following guidelines:

   a. **Actions:** Fictional characters, if they are carefully made, are subject to the same weaknesses that real people have, and when they speak, they are just as likely to exaggerate or lie. Therefore, when we want to know about characters, we have to be careful that we don't believe everything they say. We have to examine what they *do*, just as in real life we have to do more than just listen to people as they talk about themselves; we have to *watch what they do to tell what they are really like*.

   b. **Their motives:** In well-written fiction there are motives for all of the actions of the characters. Just as in real life, fictional characters do not just do things; there are reasons. How we get along in our lives is in some measure dependent on how well we understand the motives of the people with whom we interact. Actions are fairly easy to understand, but sometimes the motives behind them are hard to spot. There are two types of motives:

      1) *Internal:* These are feelings the character has, such as fear, hope, faith, greed or any anxiety or feeling.
      2) *External*: Motives based on forces outside the character, such as trees, laws or other characters.

   c. **How their relationships affect characters' actions:** All characters in fiction develop relationships just as people in life do. The choices characters make are often dictated by how they feel about other characters. It's important for readers to understand these relationships that have been created so the characters' actions will make sense and the reader will not be surprised by what choices are made. Some relationships are obvious to new readers, but these relationships are subtle and readers need to think about them. New readers have to be taught how to think about characters' actions and to relate them to relationships. This is a complicated process and will take some practice.

   d. **How their speech tells us about them:** The *way* people (characters) talk reveals a great deal about them. A careful listener/reader can judge fairly accurately what part of the country a character comes from, the amount of education that character has, how much interest the character has in other people and, in many cases, what motivates a character's actions. Young readers will have to have help for some time before they'll be able to "read" a character's speech, for this is a fairly complicated process. Noticing what characters say about themselves and what other characters say about them is another indicator of what characters are like.

e. **The kinds of people they are determines how they function:** This can determine their success with the problem of the story. The success of the protagonist in a story is, in a major way, dependent on the kinds of people involved.

f. **How their weaknesses and strengths affect their behavior:** When we deal with people we have to be aware of the ways they're strong and the ways they're weak. We then can make allowances for their weaknesses, and we can count on their strengths. The same conditions exist in fiction. It's important to try to recognize and understand the weaknesses and strengths of fictional characters.

g. **How physical characteristics affect characters' behavior:** If an author gives a character unusual characteristics, the reader should pay particular attention to that character and watch that character's actions. If an author makes all of his characters average in appearance or doesn't give physical descriptions of them at all, then they're not what the author wants the reader to concentrate on, and the physical traits of the characters don't matter to the story. Such characters' actions are often influenced by this trait or are the result of them being conscious of their appearance.

h. **How intelligence and/or schooling affect and help characters solve problems:** The better prepared people are to solve problems the more likely they are to be able to do so. This is also true in fiction. Authors decide on the intelligence and schooling of their characters before they introduce them to their readers. If an author doesn't know how smart one of the characters should be, there would be no way that author could control the abilities of that character. Sometimes that character would act brilliantly and at other times stupidly. Obviously this wouldn't be good.

B. LITERARY TERMS RELATING TO CHARACTERS

1. **Fully Developed Characters:** Have personalities which are distinctive and explained in detail and are called full dimensional or rounded-out characters. The plot centers on them, and these are the characters we get to know well. They are motivated by realistic desires, experience a full range of emotions, and interact with other characters.

2. **Flat Characters:** These are the characters who are one-dimensional; that is, we only get to know one side of their personality. They are in the story to advance the plot. Usually these are minor characters' parents, siblings, or people in the neighborhood. Flat characters often fit stereotypes, and sub-plots are sometimes built around them.

3. **Dynamic Characters:** These are fully developed characters. They undergo changes in the course of the narrative. Dynamic characters are very common in novels, but not in short stories.

4. **Static Characters:** Static characters do not change and their personalities remain the same throughout the story.

5. **Characters as Foils:** Those who are placed in a story with personalities or traits opposite others in order to make strong contrasts. *Foil* is a jeweler's term for gem settings which are used to make precious stones look bright. An author can make traits in one character stand out by contrasting them with those of another. Characters used as foils can be developed, flat, static or dynamic.

6. **Character Consistency:** This means staying within the range of the personality the author originally develops. We wouldn't expect the hero of a story to suddenly change and become weak.

7. **Dialogue:** Conversation between two or more characters or a conversation one character might have when alone. For instance, this could be one between a woman and her conscience.

8. **Personification:** The presentation of an animal or an object as if it had human characteristics (person making). "The sad sighing of the sea. . . ."

SAMPLE OBJECTIVES FOR CHARACTER STUDY

The following objectives contain questions which might lead to a Socratic discussion with your child.

1. **Identification with Characters:** Identifying the literary techniques which prompt sympathy or empathy and what the author has done to make the reader feel like, or want to be like a character, or not to feel for a character and the position that character is in.

2. **Personalizing:** Stating what the reader might do in the same situation as a character in the story. This might follow a brief discussion of what the character does in the situation. "That girl gives her balloon to that little boy who doesn't have one. I wonder why she does that. If you had been that little girl would you've given him your balloon? If you were poor and were in a park and saw a rich little girl who had a balloon, would you want her to give you her balloon?"

3. **Character Analysis:** Choosing a character from the reading and listing the actions of that character, then evaluating whether or not the character's words match the character's actions. "How does Mary treat her friend?" or, "Would you like to have a friend like her? or "Why?" or "Why not?"

4. **Motive Analysis:** Asking the child to talk about the actions of a character and then asking the child to explain why the character does those things. This is hard and you both will need to practice this. "When it's time for the family to get in the car and follow the moving van out of the driveway and to go to their new house, what does Janet do?" (She hid.) "That was a strange thing to do. That would mean that the family wouldn't be able to go. Why would she do that?" (So they couldn't leave.) "Why doesn't she want to leave?"(She'd miss her friends.) "What does this tell us about how she feels about her friends?"

5. **Recall of Comparisons:** Locating or identifying likenesses and differences among characters, places or events that are compared by the author. This will show an understanding of characters as foils.

6. **Recall of Character Traits:** Identifying or locating statements about characters which help to point out the types of people they are.

7. **Inferring Cause and Effect Relationships:** Guessing about the motives of characters and their interactions with others, and identifying situations where actions caused or affected consequences.

8. **Inferring Character Traits:** Guessing about the nature of characters on the basis of clues presented in the reading.

EXAMPLES OF SOCRATIC DIALOGUE
REGARDING CHARACTERS

1. CHARACTERS' ACTIONS

Discuss events in present tense. This will take practice for your reader to get used to. In just this first example, Reader, as most young readers do, uses past tense to talk about the actions.

Teacher: *I think Mr. Jones does some interesting things in this story. He says he's a generous man. Let's talk about the things he does that show how generous he really is.*

Reader: *He hid the candy when the boys came to visit. That's not a generous thing to do.*

Teacher: *Why do you suppose he hides the candy?*

Reader: *He didn't want to share it.*

Teacher: *I don't think that's something a generous person would do. What do you think?*

Reader: *He's stingy.*

Teacher: *But he says he's generous.*

Reader: *Then he was not only stingy, but a liar, too.*

Teacher: *Could there be another reason for him to hide the candy other than he wants it all for himself?*

Reader: *Like what?*

Teacher: *What reason do you think I tell you not to eat candy? Do you think I want it all for myself?*

Reader: *No.*

Teacher: *Then why would I do that?*

Reader: *So I won't spoil my dinner?*

Teacher: *Can you think of any other reason?*

Reader: *So much candy isn't good for my teeth?*

Teacher: *Sure, there could be lots of reasons why I tell you not to eat candy. Maybe I'm saving it for guests, or a party, or some special reason. Maybe it's for after dinner. Could there be some other reason why Mr. Jones hides the candy when the boys come to his house?*

Reader: *There was nothing in the story about any party or guests or any special reason. I think he just wanted it all for himself. Besides, it said in the story that when the boys were walking down the path from his house, he stood in the window, and he was eating candy as he watched them walk away. He was stingy no matter what he said.*

Teacher: *Good for you! You read that story very carefully. I'm proud of you.*

2. CHARACTERS' MOTIVES

The motives for acts are fairly easy for young readers to understand, but sometimes the motives are hard to spot. The following conversation demonstrates how young readers might begin to recognize motives.

Teacher: *That sure was a strange story. And what a way for that kid to act: Bobby giving all his stuff to the Goodwill.*

Reader: *I know. I don't understand what's going on at all.*

Teacher: *It's like he doesn't like all the things his father's given him.*

Reader: *Right, but we know he likes computer games. But he gives the computer away, too.*

Teacher: *Does he give the things away that he gets from his mother or his uncle?*

Reader: *No, and I don't understand why, if Bobby doesn't want gifts, he doesn't give everything away.*

Teacher: *There must be something about his father's gifts that he doesn't like.*

Reader: *There can't be. It's just a computer exactly like the one he saw in the store when his father visited the last time.*

Teacher: *And that's the one he gives away.*

Reader: *It's like Bobby gives the stuff away just because his father gives it to him. Doesn't he love his father?*

Teacher: *What do you think?*

Reader: *I think he loves him a lot and really misses him now that his parents are divorced.*

Teacher: *Do you think he'd give the computer away if his father were still living at home with his mother and him?*

Reader: *No.*

Teacher: *Then his giving the stuff away has to do with his father not living at home anymore?*

Reader: *I bet it does.*

Teacher: *Do you think Bobby's father would give him all those gifts if he were still living at home?*

Reader: *No. It says in the story that Bobby never got so many things before. So he couldn't have been given them before the divorce.*

Teacher: *Why do you suppose Bobby's father gives Bobby so much stuff now that he's not living there any more?*

Reader: *Could it be that's why? Because he's not living there?*

Teacher: *Why would that be?*

Reader: *Maybe he feels bad because he isn't living with Bobby anymore?*

Teacher: *Is there anything in the story that makes you think that Bobby's father misses living at home?*

Reader: *Sure. When he visits he goes around touching things like he misses them.*

Teacher: *Good for you! Now we have to try and understand why Bobby gives all that good stuff away.*

Reader: *It has to have something to do with his father not living at home anymore. Like the gifts are a substitute for him not being there.*

Teacher: *Good, and what does Bobby do with the substitutes?*

40

Reader:	*He gives them away. Oh!. . . He doesn't want a substitute for his father. He wants his father.*
Teacher:	*That makes sense to me.*

The previous reader has come to understand that characters in fiction act because they have reasons. This young reader may now begin to look for motives behind the actions of the people around him. If this happens, then reading has helped this young person to grow.

3. CHARACTERS' RELATIONSHIPS AND HOW THEY AFFECT CHARACTERS' ACTIONS

Some relationships are obvious to new readers, but many times these relationships are very subtle, and the readers need to think about them. New readers have to be taught how to think about characters' actions and to relate them to relationships. This is a complicated process, and the following conversation might help make it understandable.

Teacher:	*I'm not sure about Amy. She's funny with that test paper. She changes some of her friend's answers to make them wrong. That doesn't sound like something a person does to a friend's paper.*
Reader:	*I know. They're supposed to be best friends, and it's like she cheats in reverse.*
Teacher:	*How can a person cheat in reverse?*
Reader:	*You know, instead of doing something for her friend, she does something against her.*
Teacher:	*Against her?*
Reader:	*Sure, like making her answers wrong on the test. She's her friend, and if she changes the answers, she should change them to make them right.*
Teacher:	*A person should cheat for a friend? Is that what you mean?*
Reader:	*No, I don't think a person should cheat for someone else, whether they're friends or not. What I mean is, if they're friends they shouldn't try and hurt each other.*
Teacher:	*You think Amy is trying to hurt her friend?*
Reader:	*Sure, she has to be. Why else would she make her friend's answers wrong on such an important test? It might make the difference of who gets the math trophy.*
Teacher:	*Do you think Amy wants her friend to win the trophy?*
Reader:	*Of course, she says right in the story how much she wants her to win. Amy even tells her friend that she hopes she wins.*
Teacher:	*But if Amy's friend wins, then Amy can't win, and we know that Amy has had her heart set on winning that trophy for years.*
Reader:	*Does Amy reverse-cheat so that she can win the trophy for herself?*
Teacher:	*What do you think about this?*
Reader:	*I don't know. This is hard. There are two different things going on here. One is Amy has a friend she should help. The other is Amy wants to win the trophy for herself.*
Teacher:	*If Amy's friend doesn't win, do you think Amy will win?*
Reader:	*Sure. Amy and her friend are the two smartest girls in the school.*
Teacher:	*Do you think Amy knows this?*

Reader:	She has to.
Teacher:	Do you think Amy knows that her friend might beat her and win the trophy for herself?
Reader:	Sure.
Teacher:	Why do you think the author made these girls best friends?
Reader:	To make the story more complicated?
Teacher:	Yes, but why does that make it more complicated?
Reader:	Because the girls are best friends and they both want the same thing.
Teacher:	Why do you think Amy cheats-in-reverse?
Reader:	So she can win. Hey! I bet that's why Amy cries when she wins the trophy instead of laughing and smiling. I bet she feels bad about what she's done. I bet her friend really means more to her than the dumb trophy after all!

Good for Reader. This young reader has just realized that our relationships affect what we do and that this is true even in fiction. This reader will now look for relationships when trying to understand actions.

4. CHARACTERS' SPEECH

New readers will have to be worked with for some time before they'll be able to "read" a character's speech, for this is a fairly complicated process. The following dialogue will demonstrate this. (Notice that Reader has learned to discuss actions in present tense.)

Teacher:	The two boys and the old man in the story don't talk like we do. Why do you suppose that is?
Reader:	I don't know. How's it different?
Teacher:	They have an accent. This means that they must come from a different part of the country than the one we live in.
Reader:	Why do they have an accent?
Teacher:	This is just the way we have of saying that they talk differently from the way we do.
Reader:	What would they think if they'd hear us talking?
Teacher:	What do you imagine they'd say?
Reader:	That we have an accent?
Teacher:	Do you think we'd sound funny to them?
Reader:	If they sound funny to us, I bet we'd sound funny to them, too.
Teacher:	Does this mean that they're wrong in the way they talk and pronounce words?
Reader:	I don't know, maybe just different.
Teacher:	Do you think some of the things they say are wrong in the ways they say them?
Reader:	What do you mean?
Teacher:	What about that old man, Mr. Fister. He says, "I seen them starlings chasin crows 'afore this. They allus fight an scrap, an you kin hear 'em fer a long ways."
Reader:	Do crows really eat baby starlings?
Teacher:	I don't know much about crows. I know they attack other birds. They eat mice and all kinds of grain and seeds. But what about when he says, "I seen them. . ."? What does that tell us about his schooling?

Reader:	We don't say "I seen" but "I saw." Does that mean that he's not been to school?
Teacher:	We might say "I have seen." It might mean that he hasn't much schooling.
Reader:	Is he stupid?
Teacher:	No. Lots of smart people haven't been to much school. You haven't been to much school at all. Are you stupid?
Reader:	I'm too young to have been to a lot of school.
Teacher:	Do you suppose that most of the people in the place where the old man lives talk like he does?
Reader:	Sure, I bet they all do.
Teacher:	Would that be because they all are stupid?
Reader:	No. Maybe they all learned to talk that way since they were young.
Teacher:	Would you like to talk that way?
Reader:	I don't think so; I like the way I talk.

It might be good for a young reader to recognize that, when people act in ways that seem strange to us or talk in ways that are different, there might be a number of reasons for it. The place a person comes from and the experience a person has determine behavior.

5. THE KINDS OF PEOPLE CHARACTERS ARE

Since all people don't deal with life in the same ways, their makeup must be a factor. This is why the kinds of people characters are affect their success with the problem in fiction. The success of the hero in a story is, in a major way, dependent on the hero's makeup. In many stories for young readers, the heroes solve their problems by out-thinking the antagonists, and so their intelligence is an important factor.

Teacher:	It really surprised me that Janet is able to climb up that cliff. How do you suppose she gets enough courage to try that?
Reader:	She knows she has to get to the top to save her friend.
Teacher:	But, it's such a long way and she's had no experience climbing cliffs.
Reader:	She has no choice. If she doesn't do it her friend will die. She has to get to a doctor before the snake poison reaches her friend's heart. She has to do it.
Teacher:	When Janet gets to that one really hard-to-climb spot and can't find a place to put her foot to get any higher. . .I didn't think she could make it.
Reader:	I didn't either. And when she got to that overhang, I thought for sure she'd fall.
Teacher:	Do you think you'd be able to climb a cliff like that?
Reader:	I don't know. Janet sure is brave.
Teacher:	What's it mean to be brave?
Reader:	To do dangerous things.
Teacher:	Anything that is dangerous? Like lighting matches near gasoline?
Reader:	No. Brave means doing what has to be done even if it's dangerous. Lighting matches near gasoline is just stupid, not brave.
Teacher:	Would you call doing just good things brave?
Reader:	What do you mean?

Teacher:	*What if Janet's friend is not bitten by the snake? What if Janet just wants to show off by climbing the cliff. Would that be brave?*
Reader:	*No. To be brave a person has to do something because it has to be done. And this has to be for a good reason and not just to show off.*
Teacher:	*What kind of a person would Janet be if she doesn't try to climb the cliff? What if she says to her friend, "I can't climb that. I'm afraid of falling. I'll walk around even if it takes all night. You might not die."?*
Reader:	*That wouldn't be good. Her friend would die of the snake bite.*
Teacher:	*Does Janet have a choice here? Can she choose to climb or not to climb?*
Reader:	*Sure, she can not climb, but then the story would be stupid. Her friend would die and Janet would be sorry for the rest of her life.*
Teacher:	*What if Janet were to fall and break her leg? She'd lie at the bottom of the cliff with her friend and they both would die.*
Reader:	*Oh, boy. This gets complicated.*

Reader has just come to some decision about what it means to be brave from reading about a brave act. This means that these story events were made meaningful in a personal way. This is one of the benefits of reading. A reader can grow by reading and thinking about fictional characters and their actions in stories with morals. Young people learn better from examples than from directions.

6. CHARACTERS' WEAKNESSES AND STRENGTHS AND HOW THIS AFFECTS THEIR ACTIONS

It's important for young readers to recognize and understand the weaknesses and strengths of fictional characters. The following conversation should show how a young reader can be helped to understand this.

Teacher:	*It doesn't seem fair to me that Beth always gets her way with Dave. She really uses him. How do you suppose she's able to get away with that?*
Reader:	*I don't know. Every time she wants something or wants Dave to do something, he gives it to her or he does it for her. It's like Dave doesn't have a will of his own.*
Teacher:	*Or doesn't want to have one.*
Reader:	*Right. She makes him give her rides and do her homework and even do some of the cleaning at her house that her mother tells her to do.*
Teacher:	*You feel that she takes advantage of Dave?*
Reader:	*Sure she does. He's stupid to let her, too.*
Teacher:	*Why do you think he does all that for her?*
Reader:	*I don't know. All she has to do is ask him and he does it. Other kids don't do all those things when she asks.*
Teacher:	*Might there be something about Dave that makes him want to please her?*
Reader:	*I don't know what it could be. What is it?*
Teacher:	*What is there about Dave that's not true about the other kids in the story?*
Reader:	*He's just another kid.*
Teacher:	*All of the things about him are the same?*

Reader:	*Well, no. His mother's dead. She died when Dave was in the third or fourth grade. Other than that, he's like everybody else.*
Teacher:	*If that's the only thing that's different, might that have something to do with it?*
Reader:	*His mother wanted him to do things for Beth? But, that doesn't make sense. We don't even know if she knew Beth.*
Teacher:	*How does Beth act toward Dave?*
Reader:	*How do you mean?*
Teacher:	*Like a girlfriend?*
Reader:	*No. Nothing like that at all.*
Teacher:	*Like one of the guys?*
Reader:	*Not really. She doesn't behave like a guy would. She doesn't talk like one or even act like one some of the time.*
Teacher:	*How does she talk when she asks Dave to do something for her?*
Reader:	*She doesn't ask at all. She tells him what to do.*
Teacher:	*What does she sound like when she tells him to do something?*
Reader:	*Just like he's supposed to do it. Like it's his job to be doing things for her.*
Teacher:	*Who do you know who tells kids to do things like they have a right to?*
Reader:	*Kids' mothers.*
Teacher:	*But, Dave doesn't have a mother to tell him what to do.*
Reader:	*Beth sounds just like a mother when she tells him to help her, though.*
Teacher:	*And Dave does it?*
Reader:	*Just like he would if Beth were his mother.*
Teacher:	*You think Beth knows she sounds like a mother when she tells Dave to do things?*
Reader:	*She'd have to know. She doesn't talk that way to the other kids.*
Teacher:	*If Beth knows this and still does it, it must be on purpose.*
Reader:	*It's like she's taking advantage of Dave not having a mother, and she's the substitute mother he wants?*
Teacher:	*And Dave in some way is pleasing his mother by pleasing Beth?*
Reader:	*That could be. Beth knows Dave misses his mother and uses that to make him do things for her.*
Teacher:	*So you think Beth is manipulating Dave?*
Reader:	*I'm not sure, but I feel like telling Dave not to do what she wants all the time. I think she takes advantage of him not having a mother. That's really rotten.*

7. PHYSICAL CHARACTERISTICS AND HOW THEY AFFECT CHARACTERS' BEHAVIOR

What such a character does will often be influenced by the character's appearance or be a result of the character being conscious of appearance. The following conversation points this out.

Teacher:	*There sure are some strange people in that story. Almost everyone has a problem.*
Reader:	*It's a good thing that in real life there aren't so many weird people.*
Teacher:	*You think the author exaggerated too much putting them all in the same story?*

Reader:	I never met that many.
Teacher:	If there aren't so many in life, then the author must have included them all for some purpose. There must be a reason for them to be there. It might be good for us to think about this for a while.
Reader:	How will we ever know what the author had in mind?
Teacher:	We never will. But we can try and make sense out of the story even if there's no way to know what the author was thinking.
Reader:	Okay. Where do we start?
Teacher:	Let's talk about the main character, the girl who is overweight. If a character's in any way unusual, in a physical way, then the author must have planned to have the character that way and this must be for a reason.
Reader:	Why would the author want a fat girl?
Teacher:	She's unusual looking. What does she do that's unusual?
Reader:	She doesn't like boys. She says she never wants to talk to a boy and sure never wants to go out with one.
Teacher:	You find that unusual?
Reader:	Sure. The other girls in the story like boys. They all go out on dates. All except Alice.
Teacher:	You feel she doesn't like boys?
Reader:	That's what she says.
Teacher:	You think she's telling the truth?
Reader:	She doesn't have to be telling the truth. She's not the story-teller. What you call the narrative voice. She's the main character, but she doesn't talk to the reader. She just talks to other characters.
Teacher:	Does she have to tell the truth when she talks to other characters?
Reader:	Of course not. She can lie just like anybody can. Just because she's in a story doesn't mean she has to tell the truth. You told me that. In fact, we know she lies. She lies to her mother about where she goes with her girl friends.
Teacher:	So we have a character who lies. This means we can't believe for sure anything she says.
Reader:	That doesn't mean that she has to lie all the time does it?
Teacher:	No. She can tell the truth when she wants to.
Reader:	How do we know when she's lying?
Teacher:	We don't for sure. We have to be suspicious of what she says, though. Do you think she gets anything out of lying. Does it benefit her?
Reader:	She always lies to make herself look good. She tells lies about other kids. Usually the popular ones.
Teacher:	Why would she do that?
Reader:	Because she isn't popular?
Teacher:	Would lying make her popular?
Reader:	No.
Teacher:	Would it make her think the popular kids aren't so good after all?
Reader:	I think so. When she says she doesn't like boys, I know she's lying. I can tell she really wants to go out with Ron.

Teacher:	Do you think Ron likes her?
Reader:	No.
Teacher:	Do you think she knows he doesn't like her?
Reader:	Sure, she'd have to know. He ignores her, and when he doesn't, he makes fun of her being fat.
Teacher:	This must hurt her.
Reader:	It must because she secretly likes him.
Teacher:	But she says she hates all boys and wouldn't go out with one on a bet.
Reader:	She would if he asked her to go.
Teacher:	Is that likely to happen?
Reader:	No, and she knows it.
Teacher:	The author has her say that she doesn't want to go out with him. There must be a reason for this.
Reader:	I bet it's so she doesn't get disappointed that he won't ask her. She can pretend she doesn't want to go, and when he doesn't ask her, she won't be hurt.
Teacher:	That's good thinking. Why won't he ask her out?
Reader:	Because she's a big liar?
Teacher:	Then her physical condition makes her act in such a way?
Reader:	We sure figured that one out, didn't we?

8. INTELLIGENCE AND/OR SCHOOLING AND HOW THEY AFFECT RELATIONSHIPS AND HELP SOLVE PROBLEMS

It's important for young readers to have some grasp of the intelligence and education of characters in fiction. The following conversation may demonstrate one way that a young reader could be helped in this regard.

Teacher:	It was touch and go there for a while when I didn't know if the boys would get out of the woods alive or not.
Reader:	I was sure they'd die. If not of cold that first night then at least of hunger. They could be lost for a long time.
Teacher:	How smart do you think those boys are?
Reader:	Boy, that's a tough question. At first I thought the city boy would be real dumb in the woods, but he's the one who saves them that first night.
Teacher:	What made you think he'd be ignorant about the woods?
Reader:	He comes from the big city. He's never been in a large woods before. He has only city clothes on, and he talks like he doesn't know anything about the forest.
Teacher:	Do you think the author does this on purpose?
Reader:	Does what?
Teacher:	Leads you to think that the city boy is ignorant in the woods.
Reader:	Sure, it has to be on purpose.
Teacher:	Why would an author do that?
Reader:	To get the reader thinking that the boys won't be able to survive that first night.
Teacher:	Why would an author want a reader to think that?

Reader: So we'd worry about the boys.

Teacher: Right. He creates suspense if he can make the reader think they won't make it. Are we made to think the country boy is smart or stupid?

Reader: Everybody talks about how much the country boy knows about the woods and survival and all. We think the country boy is so much smarter than the city boy, and if the boys do get lost, the country boy'll be able to save them.

Teacher: But that's not what happens, is it?

Reader: No. When the boys do get lost, it's the city boy who knows enough to keep them alive.

Teacher: What do you think this story's about?

Reader: Being smart and knowing lots of stuff is good. At least that's what happens.

Teacher: What about irony here?

Reader: Irony? What's that again?

Teacher: Irony is when the unexpected happens. When there is a reversal of anticipated actions.

Reader: That sounds complicated, but I do see the opposite of what I expected.

Teacher: Tell me about it.

Reader: I expected that the country boy would know all about survival in the woods at night with no tent or matches or food or anything like that. But it's the city boy who knows what to do from reading books about adventurers and how they survive. I expected the city boy would be the one to be scared and panic and try to find the way out of the forest. But, he's the one who decides that they should stay put and let the others find them. It's the right thing to do, and, because he knows that, they're okay.

Once again, an assessment of the characteristics of characters helps a reader understand a story. What Teacher and Reader decide here is not necessarily what the writer had in mind, but if it makes sense, it allows the reader to enjoy the fiction more once a feeling for the abilities of the characters is realized.

III. CONFLICT

Characters in stories will always have conflicts. There is an old saying, "If there isn't a problem, there isn't a story." Conflicts are the forces in a story acting against each other. Before writing, a writer makes a decision about the *nature* of the conflict in the story, what the *forces* in the conflict will be, and what each *character's involvement* will be in it.

There will always be two "sides" of conflict or forces or characters in a story: the **protagonist,** who may be the hero or main character, and the **antagonist,** who is the force or character which is against or wants to stop the protagonist from succeeding. Young readers may simply define these sides as "good" and "bad."

In order for the conflict to create suspense, *the strengths of the two sides of the conflict must differ*. If a professional football team (the protagonist force) were to have a game against a local high school team (the antagonist force), this would not be much of a conflict, and the reader would not worry about the "good" professional team being beaten. On the other hand, if the high school team is the protagonist force and opposes a team of superior ability (the antagonist), there could be much suspense. This is why the heroes in children's stories are very often alone or do not have adults (parents) to help them. They must overcome great odds and trick or outwit very powerful opposing forces or characters to be successful or to get what they want.

A. UNDERSTANDING CONFLICTS

1. **The nature of the forces:** This will determine the type of conflict that takes place. It will be either **internal** or **external conflict.**

    a. **Internal conflict:** This is a conflict that takes place within a character, such as a guilty conscience. The reader must focus on the character with this problem and what the character's desires are (the **protagonist** force) and the opposition (the **antagonist** force) that is trying to keep those desires from being satisfied.

    b. **External conflict:** A conflict that is between a character and some outside force, such as nature. For a reader to make sense of a story, both the character and the outside force must be understood. The reader must focus on these two forces as the external antagonist force tries to defeat the desires of the protagonist character.

2. **By the situation:** There are four types of conflict which the protagonist may face: against person, against nature, against society, or against self.

    a. **Person against Person:** In many stories the conflict is between two of the main characters, the *protagonist and the antagonist*. In this type of conflict, these two forces are made up of one or more characters who are pitted against each other. An understanding of these two forces and the conflicts will lead readers to a recognition of the central ideas of many stories.

Stories for young readers may have animals who are struggling against each other. In a person against person conflict they'll want the same thing, and the conflict (struggle) is over which one will get it. It can be over a person such as a best friend, or objects like a bike, a tree house, or hat, or it could be over an intangible thing like an idea.

b. **Person against Nature:** In a person against nature conflict, one character (or group of children or animals) has a struggle with elements of nature. Many adventure stories are written with this major conflict. This often is the ocean, the cold of winter, a storm, flood, fire or wind. The story of man's struggle against these large natural forces is fascinating, and young readers particularly enjoy these contests.

In order for this type of conflict to be meaningful for a young reader, the nature of the natural force must be understood. Some writers assume that their readers will understand conditions such as hypothermia or dehydration or how easy it is to become disoriented in a forest, but this is not always the case. If the characteristics of the natural force are not explained in a story, it would be difficult for young readers to appreciate the story.

Examples of this kind of conflict for young readers might be to make a raft to float on a pond, climb a tall hill, have a picnic on a rainy day, create an ice skating rink when there is no water, find a honey tree, or any of hundreds of other situations in which young characters could find themselves.

c. **Person against Society:** A popular conflict is with a person against a group of people who are in control. Often this group is called society, and it may be represented by school teachers and administrators, city government workers, neighborhood council members, the church leadership or members of a club or organization.

Young readers need to understand the dynamics of a group and the power groups have. In a person against society conflict, one character is in a struggle with a group with which that member belongs. This could be a person or animal who doesn't want to do what the group thinks is best or right to do. This character might not want to build a clubhouse, start an animal hospital in the neighborhood, go swimming at night or pick on an unfortunate neighbor.

d. **Person against Self:** Some stories are written so that the main character has what is called an internal conflict, one between two forces within a character.

This will involve what we call "better judgment" or "conscience" or moral or religious training. The character wants to do something that is hard to resist or to accomplish something which is known to be wrong. Young readers need help with this type of conflict.

A person against self conflict might be with a desire to eat more than is healthy and the knowledge that this is not a good thing to do, a desire to have something even if it means to steal it and the knowledge that stealing is wrong, a feeling of guilt over something that has been done, a fear of doing something that has to be done, or where a character must or must not do something.

3. **By the progression of the plot:** Once the **setting** is established and the **characters** are introduced, the conflict begins to unfold through a series of events. In many stories there are also **sub plots** which often tie in with the main plot at some point and add interest and action. Although every story is different, the conflict format is fairly consistent and will progress in a sequence which looks something like this:

   a. **Situation:** The forces in the story are defined.

   b. **Inciting Force:** Actions occur which trigger the conflict. This doesn't have to be a major move or an important event. Some small thing might set off the conflict. At this point the sides are drawn and the rules of the conflict are set.

   c. **Rising Action:** The conflict gains momentum. Now the forces in conflict are unstoppable in their struggle. The forces (desires of the characters) take over the action and drive the story to its conclusion.

   d. **Crisis:** The point in the story when the struggle is at its height. There can be no retreat of the participants. At this time there can be nothing but the clash of the forces as they face each other for the showdown. One side must lose and one must win. There can be no "draw." They are driven to the climax.

   e. **Climax:** The place in the action at which it's possible to tell the outcome of the conflict. One side must be seen to be in the position of the loser and one the winner. All of the abilities of both sides have been brought to bear on the conflict and the outcome is determined.

   f. **Resolution:** Wraps up all loose ends in a story and answers all remaining questions.

4. **By the factors that affect conflict:**

   a. **The kinds of people they are affect their success with the problem of the story.** The success of the protagonist in a story is, in a major way, dependent on the

51

kinds of people involved. In many stories for young readers the protagonists solve their problems by out-thinking the antagonists.

b. **The intelligence and/or schooling of the characters determines how they solve problems.** The better prepared people are to solve problems, the more likely they are to be able to do so. This is also true in fiction. Authors decide on the intelligence and schooling of their characters before they introduce them to their readers. If an author doesn't know how smart a character should be, there would be no way that author could control the abilities of that character. Sometimes that character would act brilliantly and at other times stupidly.

B. SAMPLE OBJECTIVES RELATING TO STUDY OF CONFLICT

1. **Identifying the major forces of conflict in the story:** These are the **protagonist** and **antagonist** forces. For young readers, using the terms "good guy" and "bad guy" might be helpful.

2. **Sequencing the steps of the conflict:** In doing this, older readers might use the correct literary terms such as, *Conflict, Inciting Force, Rising Action, Crisis, Climax,* and *Resolution.* Asking young readers what happened first, second, and so on might be easier for them to understand.

3. **Foreshadowing:** Asking the reader to identify foreshadowing in the text.

4. **Forecasting (Predicting):** Asking the reader to tell what will happen next. These questions should be preceded by a short review of the immediate events up to that time. "All the kids come to the party except Janet. What do you think will be the reason for Janet's not going to the party?" or, "The bear comes right into the camp and walks into the tent. Do you think that bear will find the food in the box?"

5. **Personalizing:** Asking the reader to describe what he or she might do if faced with the same problem.

6. **Motives:** Asking the reader to determine the reasons behind the conflict and whether or not it was preventable.

7. **Cause & Effect Relationships:** Asking the reader to identify cause and effect relationships that affect the conflict. "The girl's trouble starts when she climbs out of her bedroom window."

8. **Plots and Sub Plots:** Asking the reader to identify the plot progression (the sides of the conflict, inciting force, rising action, crisis, climax and resolution). Reader might also identify the sub plots in the story.

EXAMPLES OF SOCRATIC DIALOGUE REGARDING CONFLICT

Conflict can be understood best by examining elements such as the following:

1. **PERSON AGAINST PERSON**

An understanding of these two forces and the conflicts will lead young readers to a recognition of the central ideas of many stories. Readers can be helped with this understanding, as seen in the following conversation.

Teacher: *In this story Janet does some things that I'm not too sure are very clear.*

Reader: *It's a hard one to understand what the author's getting at. Everything works out in the end, but what's the conflict?*

Teacher: *Let's look at what happens and that may help. Who do you see as the hero or the protagonist in this story?*

Reader: *Janet.*

Teacher: *Who is the "bad guy" or the antagonist?*

Reader: *The dog who digs and makes a mess in Janet's mother's flowers.*

Teacher: *Do you see that dog as being intentionally bad or is the dog just doing dog-like things?*

Reader: *The dog is just being natural and doing what dogs do.*

Teacher: *Do you feel that the neighbor has a responsibility to keep her dog out of Janet's mother's flowers?*

Reader: *Sure, it's her dog and she has to take care of it.*

Teacher: *But that neighbor is Janet's mother's best friend. And she really loves that dog. So does Janet's mother. What is Janet's problem here?*

Reader: *She has to stop the dog from digging and not upset her mother or the neighbor. She sure doesn't want to cause a problem between the two women over the dog.*

Teacher: *Does Janet have a problem with her mother?*

Reader: *No, her mother doesn't even know it's the dog that's killing her flowers.*

Teacher: *Does Janet have an internal problem?*

Reader: *What's that again?*

Teacher: *Is the conflict within Janet? Is there something in her that is in conflict with another part of her?*

Reader: *Give me an example.*

Teacher: *Will Janet feel guilty if she stops the dog from coming over to her mother's flowers every morning when the neighbor lady lets it out?*

Reader: *No. She'd only feel guilty if she does something to upset the friendship. That's why she has to be so careful. That neighbor thinks her little dog is perfect and wouldn't do anything wrong. She'd be really upset if Janet were to say anything against that dog.*

Teacher: *Does Janet have a problem with the dog? Is there anything she can do to change how the dog acts? Could the dog be the antagonist?*

Reader: No. The dog is just being a dog. Of course, she doesn't want to hurt the dog, and she doesn't want to say anything to the neighbor lady, and she can't call the dog pound to pick the dog up for being out without a leash, because then the neighbor lady would know who it was who called.

Teacher: Good. Janet does a strange thing with the metal posts and the wire. If this solves the problem, then all we have to figure out is who the action with the wire is aimed at.

Reader: For the dog. . .No, that's not right, because what she makes won't work. It has to be for the lady, because the dog would never be able to figure out what the posts and the wire are for. Janet wouldn't be able to explain to the dog. And anyway, the battery's no good. It says that right in the story. So there's no way the dog would get a shock and learn to stay out of the flowers. They can't be for the dog.

Teacher: Do you think it's wrong for Janet to let the neighbor lady think the wires connected to the metal posts and the battery are to scare away moles?

Reader: Janet doesn't lie, but she does talk about something killing the flowers and the grass, and that part sure is true. She doesn't say anything about the battery or the wires at all. Janet just makes sure the neighbor sees her putting the posts in the ground and stringing the wire from the posts to the battery.

Teacher: She lets the neighbor come to her own conclusion?

Reader: Sure.

Teacher: Then Janet's saying something to the lady but not in words. She's telling her something about the flowers but not talking about the dog or the wires?

Reader: Sure—Oh, I see. The conflict's between Janet and the neighbor lady, but the lady doesn't know it. Tricky!

This young reader has come to an understanding of this story by analyzing the conflict between two major characters: person against person.

2. PERSON AGAINST NATURE

Many adventure stories are written with the conflict between a person and nature. In order for this type of a conflict to be meaningful for a young reader, the nature of the natural force must be understood, or if not, the conditions of the conflict should be explained. The following conversation shows one method of doing this.

Reader: I liked that story. Jake sure was lost though, wasn't he?

Teacher: That was the point of the story, Jake being lost and how he works his way back to the road and civilization. If he doesn't find his way out, what'll happen?

Reader: He'll die.

Teacher: The conflict here is easy to spot, isn't it?

Reader: Sure, between Jake and the forest. There's one thing I don't understand, though. Why does Jake keep walking in circles?

Teacher: How do you know he does?

Reader: When he thinks he's been in that part of the forest before, he breaks a limb on a tree and the next day he comes across a tree with a broken limb.

54

Teacher:	*You think it's the same tree?*
Reader:	*If it's not the same one, why would the author put it in the story? Remember when you said that the author helps us to look at things that are important?*
Teacher:	*Good for you. The tree very well may be the same one. At least, we're made to think it might be. If it is, what's the author telling us?*
Reader:	*That Jake has been there before.*
Teacher:	*But, why tell us that?*
Reader:	*That's part of the conflict. Jake is lost and trying to walk out of the woods, but he's walking in circles. Now, why would he want to do that?*
Teacher:	*What makes you think he wants to?*
Reader:	*All he has to do is walk in a straight line and eventually he'll come to the logging road.*
Teacher:	*I've a feeling that's what Jake's trying to do.*
Reader:	*Walk in a straight line?*
Teacher:	*Yes.*
Reader:	*I don't get it. Why does he walk in a circle then?*
Teacher:	*That's part of the natural force Jake is pitted against.*
Reader:	*Explain that, please.*
Teacher:	*In the woods or on the desert, when a person's walking and there's no sun or any way to know which way is which, that person almost always walks in a big circle. This is because most people have one leg which is a little bit stronger than the other one. When lost, the person doesn't know it, but each push with the stronger leg turns that person a little bit to one side. Eventually those little pushes are enough to turn that walker right around in a very big circle.*
Reader:	*That's what must happen to Jake. Turning is one of the things he has to guard against, isn't it?*
Teacher:	*You're right again.*
Reader:	*I wonder how a person could keep from doing that.*

This young reader, now that one of the forces the protagonist must overcome is understood, has a much better grasp on the nature of the conflict.

3. **PERSON AGAINST SOCIETY**

A popular conflict is with a person against a group of people who are in control. The young reader must understand the dynamics of the group and the power groups have. The following conversation is about this subject.

Reader:	*I don't understand why Rafe gives up and goes back to the gang at the end of that story. Why doesn't he just stay away and be by himself?*
Teacher:	*There are some advantages to him being a member of that group aren't there?*
Reader:	*Sure, they have lots of food and they can protect themselves because there's so many of them. They can raid the old stores that've been abandoned and find canned vegetables and peaches. They all like peaches.*

Teacher:	Is there any other benefit to being in a group?
Reader:	There are people to talk to. And when some are sick the rest can take care of them. And they can give each other hope that they'll be found.
Teacher:	Those are all practical reasons for Rafe returning to the group. If Rafe could have all of these things, is there any other reason why he'd want to go back?
Reader:	He gets lonely.
Teacher:	Sure he does. What does being lonely mean?
Reader:	He wants to be with other people.
Teacher:	Is this natural?
Reader:	Sure. Everyone wants to be with people. That's the way people are.
Teacher:	Good. If it's natural for a person to want to be with other people, there must be a drive in each of us to belong to groups, to want to be together.
Reader:	I think so. That's one of the things pulling on Rafe. He wants to be with other people even though it would be dangerous. He knows this but he still goes back to be with them. He has to fight not just the group but his own loneliness.
Teacher:	Good thinking. That's a powerful force, isn't it?
Reader:	It sure is for Rafe.

4. PERSON AGAINST SELF

Some stories are written so that the main character has what is called an internal conflict. This is with what we call "better judgment" or "conscience" or moral or religious training. The character wants to do something known to be wrong or has done something and now feels guilty about it. Young readers need help with this type of conflict. The following conversation shows how one reader receives this help.

Teacher:	There's a strange twist to this story. What do you think of it?
Reader:	Are you asking about Mekog tipping his sled over and getting the dogs tangled up?
Teacher:	Yes. After all he does to win, then he loses. That's interesting for the author to have it end that way. Let's look at what he does to win.
Reader:	Some of the things he does aren't so good.
Teacher:	Like what?
Reader:	He switches dogs. He makes everybody think he'll be using his own dogs in the race, but when he hitches them up to the sled, he hitches up two of his uncle's dogs.
Teacher:	You feel that's wrong?
Reader:	Sure, it's wrong. The race is supposed to be between boys and the dogs they've trained, and he hasn't trained any of his uncle's dogs. His uncle has, and he's a professional dog trainer. What Mekog does is cheating.
Teacher:	Why do you think Mekog does this?
Reader:	To win, of course.
Teacher:	He wants to win very badly?

Reader:	He needs the new sled that goes to the winner. Early in the story he tells his friend that he'll do almost anything for the sled. And he does. He even goes to the other boy's house and scrapes the wax off of the runners on his sled.
Teacher:	Why does he do that?
Reader:	So the sled won't slide easily on the snow.
Teacher:	So he can win the race?
Reader:	Sure.
Teacher:	You feel he does some very wrong things in this race then.
Reader:	He sure does.
Teacher:	Do you think Mekog knows these things are wrong to do?
Reader:	He has to know. He sneaks when he does them. If he didn't feel guilty about them, then he wouldn't have to sneak.
Teacher:	Where did he learn that those things are not right to do?
Reader:	He's been trained to race by his uncle who's a champion racer. He's been told what's right and what not to do. That's how he knows to scrape off the wax. His uncle had told him about a man who won a race by doing that.
Teacher:	But then he tips over his sled on the hill and the other boy passes him. By the time he gets the sled upright, he's so far behind he loses the race.
Reader:	It's almost as if he does it on purpose.
Teacher:	Why do you say that?
Reader:	Mekog is too good a sled racer to tip his sled over accidentally. He has to want to lose. But why?
Teacher:	At first he wants to win, and then during the race he wants to lose?
Reader:	It's like he changes his mind about winning.
Teacher:	If that's true, then something happens between the start of the race and when he decides to lose.
Reader:	The only thing that happens is that his uncle can get to the race after all.
Teacher:	Do you think that Mekog thinks his uncle will recognize his dogs?
Reader:	No. He's too far away and can't get close enough to see that well. All Mekog does is see him sitting in his pickup truck.
Teacher:	That's enough?
Reader:	I think so. I bet Mekog begins to feel guilty when he sees his uncle. That's why he tips over his sled on the hill. He feels bad about what he's done to win. Now he has to lose.
Teacher:	What do you think are the forces in conflict in this story?
Reader:	I thought it was with Mekog and the other boy in the race, but now I know it's Mekog and his guilt.
Teacher:	Is it a better story now than before?
Reader:	It's the same story, but I like it better.

IV. RESOLUTION

A. **UNDERSTANDING THE RESOLUTION:** After the conflict has reached its climatic point and the outcome of the struggle is apparent, there is a time of "falling action," and then the resolution. The resolution of a story is the consequence of the conflict climax. This means that when the conflict is resolved the story ends. What we call story resolution is that part of the story after the climax produces a winner and loser to the conflict. In this part of narration, all questions are answered and subplots are resolved.

B. **LITERARY TERMS/SKILLS RELATING TO RESOLUTION:**

1. **Falling Action:** The conflict has lost momentum and the story is coming to its end.

2. **Denouement:** Older students might call this portion of the story the "denouement," a French word meaning "outcome or result." For young readers, calling it the "ending" or "conclusion" is fine.

C. **SAMPLE OBJECTIVES FOR UNDERSTANDING RESOLUTION:**

1. **Examining the Resolution:** Discuss with your child the ending of the story. Give to your child the idea that stories might end in lots of different ways and still be good stories. It stimulates a child to think creatively about what might have been.

2. **Foreshadowing and the Resolution:** Look again at the story and discuss the author's use of foreshadowing that hinted that things would end as they do.

EXAMPLE OF SOCRATIC DIALOGUE
REGARDING RESOLUTION

Reader: *That ending was sad, wasn't it?*
Teacher: *Does that surprise you?*
Reader: *Aren't there supposed to be happy endings to stories?*
Teacher: *Not always.*
Reader: *Why not?*
Teacher: *That's not the way life is. Things don't always turn out the way you want them to. In fact, it can't be like that.*
Reader: *Why not?*
Teacher: *What might make one character happy could make another character unhappy.*
Reader: *Who would be unhappy if the wolf cub stayed there on the ranch with them?*
Teacher: *The wolf?*
Reader: *But they had to scare the wolf off when it was grown. It wanted to stay with them, didn't it?*

Teacher:	It sure seemed like it, but you have to understand what wolves are like. They're not like big dogs. They're wild animals, even if they're raised by people. They are only happy in the wild with their own kind.
Reader:	Then the story had a happy ending?
Teacher:	Not for Nick it doesn't, does it?
Reader:	No. It said he has tears in his eyes when the wolf runs into the forest.
Teacher:	I think his father has them, too.
Reader:	Everybody can't always be happy at the end of every story, can they?
Teacher:	No, and that's the way life is, too. The end for some is just the beginning for others.

V. POINT OF VIEW

Point of view gets fairly complicated, so some explanation may be needed. For your young reader the terms *first* and *third person* and *present* and *past tense* are enough of a challenge and sufficient for understanding stories, but older readers must comprehend much more about the nature of the narrative voice. Below is a chart and an explanation of the choices an author has in creating a voice.

Older readers need to understand all the point of view choices presented here since an author's selection of point of view is necessary to the understanding of any fiction.

You may have to work with this section many times before your children feel comfortable with it. That's fine. You've got years to work with them, and you can come back to this section as often as you're comfortable with it.

All good writers make at least the following selections before they begin to write, and good readers recognize these elements. Note the chart on the next page.

POINT OF VIEW OPTIONS

Person:	First Singular or Plural	Second "you"	Third Singular or Plural
Tense:	Past	Present	Future
Attitude:	Objective		Subjective
Involvement:	Part of Action		Observer
Knowledge:	Limited Omniscient	Restricted to Observation	Restricted to Participation
Perspective:	Omnipresent Overview		Restricted to Personal View

DEFINITION OF POINT OF VIEW OPTIONS

PERSON

FIRST:

This is the narrative voice in which the writer refers to himself and speaks directly to the reader.

FIRST SINGULAR:

The narrator, in his capacity as story teller, refers to himself as an individual and not as part of a group by the use of *I*.

FIRST PLURAL:

The narrator, although speaking to the reader as an individual, constantly refers to himself as part of a group, using *We*.

THIRD SINGULAR:

The narrative voice refers to one character at a time and talks about groups of people only in the sense of them being observed by one individual: *He saw the flag. She saw the people in the parade.*

TIIIRD PLURAL:

The narrative voice always talks about a group of two or more people, using *they* or *them*.

TENSE

PAST:

The narrative voice talks about things which occurred in the past.

PRESENT:

The narrative voice refers to actions as if they were happening at the time he is telling about them.

FUTURE:

The narrative voice tells about things which will happen in the future.

ATTITUDE

OBJECTIVE:

This voice shows no emotional involvement in the actions in the narration. It seems to have no attitude about the characters or what they do, and assumes almost a scientific objectivity about the events.

SUBJECTIVE:

This voice cares about the characters and what they do and lets the reader know this by making comments indicating it has made value judgements.

INVOLVEMENT

PART OF ACTION:

The narrative voice is one of the characters who takes a part in the events in either a main or supporting role.

OBSERVER:

The narrative voice watches the action from some removed vantage point. It is never a participator, rather a viewer of events.

KNOWLEDGE

LIMITED OMNISCIENT:

This voice has a wide range of possibilities. It can be in more than one mind and know what is happening in many places. It has an expanded view of the action.

RESTRICTED TO OBSERVATION:

This voice has a narrow view as if it were speaking from knowledge gained by looking at the action in the house next door.

RESTRICTED TO PARTICIPATION:

The narrative voice is part of the action and can't know what is happening in other places, or know what happens to other characters when it is not with them.

PERSPECTIVE

OMNIPRESENT OVERVIEW:

The narrative voice must have some form of omniscience, for it can describe things in two places at one time and take the reader into the past and future and can show the reader the actions from any angle or from any vantage point it chooses.

RESTRICTED TO PERSONAL VIEW:

The narrative voice assumes the position of a person in the story either as a participant or an observer. This view is limited to what a real person could see, hear and know.

On the next pages are some examples of these points of view as they operate in sentences:

PERSON: First and Third, Singular and Plural:

First person singular: *I saw* the dog.
Third person singular: *He saw* the dog.
First person plural: *We saw* the dog.
Third person plural: *They saw* the dog.

TENSE: Past - Present - Future:

First singular, past: *I saw* the dog.
Third plural, past: *They saw* the dog.

First singular, present: *I see* the dog.
Third plural, present: *They see* the dog.

First singular, future: *I will see* the dog.
Third plural, future: *They will see* the dog.

ATTITUDE: Objective - Subjective:

First person, singular, past, objective: I saw *the hungry dog*. (Note that the narrative voice gives no indication of how it feels about seeing a hungry animal.)

Third person plural, future, subjective: They will see *the poor* hungry dog.

INVOLVEMENT: Part of action (central or peripheral), Observer (minimal or non-involved):

First person, singular, past, subjective, central to action: I felt sorry for the poor, hungry dog when *I had to chase it away* from the door.

Third person, singular, past, objective, non-involved: *He watched the cook chase* the hungry dog away from the kitchen doorway.

First person, plural, past, subjective, minimally involved: *We held the door* so the cook could chase away the poor, hungry dog.

KNOWLEDGE: Limited omniscient, restricted to participation and restricted to observation:

Third person, past, subjective, non-involved, observer, limited omniscient: It was a cruel thing that the boys should have to hold the door *when they felt so sorry* for the lonely and hungry dog that the cook, *who really hated all animals*, chased away from the back of the trash-filled alley.

First person, present, objective, minimally involved, knowledge restricted to action: *Opening the door for the cook*, I see the hungry dog and *watch through the crack in the hinge line* as the cook throws a rock and chases it away.

First person plural, past, subjective, non-involved, knowledge restricted to observation: *From our room over the alley we looked down on the back of the restaurant* and there saw the two boys hold the door for the cruel cook so he could throw stones at the poor dog.

PERSPECTIVE: Omnipresent overview and Limited to personal view:

Third person, past, objective, non-involved, limited omniscient, omnipresent overview: *The dog had been in the alley happily rooting in the garbage only a short time* when the two not-very-bright boys opened the door, and the cook, who never had liked dogs, threw stones, and the *frightened dog ran down to the corner and into the alley in the next block where it found better pickings anyway.*

SKILLS AND OBJECTIVES FOR UNDERSTANDING POINT OF VIEW

An understanding of the choices an author has in selecting the characteristics of his narrative voice doesn't involve memorizing the definitions of the choices. That won't help.

There are many exercises in the *Writing Strands* books that teach how to control point of view, and this should be sufficient training in this skill. If you're not using *Writing Strands* (shame on you), then you should take the time to have discussions often about this aspect of narration. It's important to the understanding of literature.

When your children have had repeated experiences discussing these elements, you'll find that they remember them and memory work won't be necessary. They should understand the following things about point of view:

1. They should be able to tell others what choices an author has in creating a narrative voice and be able to give examples of each one.

2. They should be able to identify in any passage of narration what choices the author has made for the narrative voice and explain how they can recognize them.

3. They should be able to identify in their own writing the point of view elements they have chosen to use.

4. They should be able talk to you about the effect a particular choice of point of view has on a piece of narration.

EXAMPLE OF SOCRATIC DIALOGUE
REGARDING POINT OF VIEW

Teacher: *That was an interesting story for me. For you, too?*

Reader: *Sure. I liked it.*

Teacher: *What did you think of Rob and what he says about his car?*

Reader: *You mean how he gets it?*

Teacher: *Yes. He tells his friends that his father had given it to him.*

Reader: *But he hadn't.*

Teacher: *We know that, but his friends don't.*

Reader: *We know he's not telling the truth because we know who he gets the car from.*

Teacher: *Let's talk about how the author selects his point of view and what this does to the story.*

Reader: *Sure, it's first person and past tense.*

Teacher: *What's that mean about what the narrative voice knows?*

Reader: *The narrative voice is Rob. . . .What's the question?*

Teacher: *Okay, Rob is telling us the story in past tense. He tells us where he gets the car, then when he's telling us about when he's with his friends, he gives us some direct dialogue.*

Reader: *We know his mother bought the car for him, but he tells us that he tells his friends that his father gave it to him. He must know that we won't believe him.*

Teacher: *Would it have been a different story if Rob hadn't been the narrative voice?*

Reader: *Would that voice lie to us?*

Teacher: *If that voice had been another character in the story, it could lie.*

Reader: *Does that mean that we can never believe what we read?*

Teacher: *You'll have to learn that characters in stories can lie to the readers if they're the narrative voices.*

Reader: *Who doesn't lie then?*

Teacher: *If the narrative voices aren't characters, you can trust what they tell you.*

Reader: *Do all characters who are narrative voices lie about what happens?*

Teacher: *No. It's just like real life. Some people lie and some you can trust. You have to develop the skill to tell the difference.*

Reader: *We have to be careful when the narrative voice in a story is a character then, don't we?*

Teacher: *Just like in life.*

EXTRA HELP WITH MEANING
FOR YOUNG AND BEGINNING READERS

It's not uncommon to hear, "I read it again, but I still don't understand." The problem of making meaning (sense) out of a writing is not very great for us, but for a beginner it's sometimes overwhelming. We all learn things at different rates. Very bright people sometimes have trouble with making sense out of words. When I was in the early grades in school, I had what was called "a reading problem." I went to special reading classes. My friends called me dumb. This hurt. I wasn't dumb, I just didn't start to understand when most of the rest of the kids did. I'm sure that many of those friends are reading at about the same level now as they were then.

If your reader needs extra help, don't worry. Be glad that you're there and want to help. The more help you can give, the better will be your relationship. I was always glad when my son needed my help. What a good feeling to give help to someone you love.

For those of us who have been doing it for a long time, the process of reading has lost some of its mystery, and, unless we think about it, has become an automatic process. But, for the very young, reading can be almost magical. Think of the wonder in a child's mind when it's first discovered that those strange black marks in a book are words and that they have meaning.

We forget how difficult it was to understand what someone else meant when we read what that person had written. The mystery in reading is not something that's bad; in fact, it's one of the wonderful things about it. I'm not suggesting that you disenchant your young reader. Rather, that you expand your reader's ability to understand the wonder.

The following exercises will help your child construct meaning from a text because it will help with *the transmission of ideas* in all the categories listed. They are only models, so read through them and decide on specific ideas (words that you'd like to use in addition to or in place of those in the examples) to use with your child.

ANALOGIES

Don't force this one. If your reader doesn't understand how this works, wait. This exercise teaches that words are related to each other. When this is understood, the reader has to see that two other words can have a similar relationship. This works like this:

1. *Big* is to *little* as *tall* is to   _____.
2. *Full* is to *empty* as *fat* is to   _____.
3. *Knife* is to *cut* as *pencil* is to _____.
4. *Cat* is to *mouse* as *spider* is to _____.

Sometimes the relationships can be very subtle, and some people just can never see the subtlety. Other people are very good at seeing relationships, and this is an easy exercise for them. Whichever is the case with your reader, this exercise will help with meanings and the logic of relationships well into the teen years.

ANTONYMS

These are words that have opposite meanings. In this exercise you are to give one word and your young reader is to give a word that means the opposite. This works like this:

1. big—little
2. good—bad
3. light—dark
4. sideways—gotcha!

CAUSE AND EFFECT

It's important that a reader understand the relationship that words have because one condition causes another. To help your reader see this relationship, you should create a sentence that has a cause and effect relationship in it and have your reader tell you why what happened did happen.

"I forgot to water the plant and it died."

You are to ask your reader: "Why did the plant die?"

This seems fairly simple. And it is, but this can be confusing to a very young reader. What appears obvious to us may be an entirely new experience for a child and not clear at all. But, watch this one, the cause and effect relationship can be tricky. In the following exercise, the sentence is fairly complicated and the cause and effect relationship is not so clear. Try this one yourself.

The fat but short candle, guttering alone there on the dirty table, even though casting dancing shadows on the walls, did not light the surface of the pages well enough for Paul to read the wrinkled map, and, twisting the map to see better, he touched its corner to the flame—which quickly ignited, burning the only place on the whole map which named the town the treasure was near.

Here are some potential reasons why Paul couldn't find the treasure:
- The map was made of burnable material.
- Paul burnt the map.
- The candle was not bright enough.
- Paul didn't make a copy like he should have.
- Paul didn't bring a flashlight.

- Paul wasn't careful enough when he read.
- Paul had poor eyesight.
- The map maker put the town's name on only one place on the map.
- John didn't change the bulb in the lamp when it burnt out, so the candle had to be lit.
- Ron didn't offer to read the map like he should have; he has good eyesight.
- It was fate!

CLASSIFICATION

This exercise is designed to teach your reader to arrange objects into groups that have similar characteristics. For instance, two and four legged animals: "Put the following animals into two groups: one for two legged animals and one for four legged animals: chicken, duck, cow, man, mouse, monkey, cat."

As your reader gets older and better at classification, this exercise can become fairly sophisticated. For instance: "Classify the following objects into three groups: airplane, boat, roller skate, ski, trampoline, car, canoe, swing, roller-coaster."

This can be turned into a game that the whole family can enjoy together, and all the children can learn this important skill at the same time.

CONTEXT AS CLUE

Now that your reader understands that a word might have a number of meanings, it must be understood how to figure out a reasonable or intended meaning. This can be done by a study of the context (the ideas presented before and after the word). Notice how you can tell the meaning from context in these two examples: "The grocer said he'd *knock down* the price," and "The grocer said he'd *knock down* the price sign." In one instance the words *knock down* mean to cut or reduce, and in the other they mean to turn over or push over.

In this exercise your reader should learn to determine meaning from context. This should start fairly simply, but as you both get used to it, you can make it as complicated as you like. You should write/speak a sentence with a word in it that is not used in its usual way. Your reader then must tell you what the word means in that context.

"Uncle George said he'd try and put a good *face* on it."
"Make it look good."

"Bill said he'd *drop over*."
"Come to our house."

"That car is really a *lemon*"
"I don't know, could it be a yellow car?"

DEFINITION

A good mental exercise for training young readers to understand meanings is to teach them to define words. A good definition has two parts. The first part establishes the general category of the word, and the second part gives some specific information that clearly identifies the object. An example of this is a definition for *jackknife*. A jackknife is a cutting instrument (general category) small enough to carry in a pocket and has a blade which folds into its handle (two specific characteristics which identify it).

In this exercise you supply the word and your reader defines it using a two-part definition. Taking turns with this one can be fun. You can have your reader give you a word, and you can define it. Both experiences will help your reader understand words better. You might have to give a good deal of help at first. That's okay, your reader will catch on. Other examples of this exercise are:

Pickup truck

General: truck
Specific: small open bed behind cab

Garbage can

General: container
Specific: designed for trash

DIFFERENCES AND SIMILARITIES

The object of this exercise is to help your young reader understand that things/words can be similar and yet be different both at the same time. You're to give two words and your reader is to tell how the two objects or words are different and similar. An example will help me make this clear.

1. *Dog* and *Cat*
   Similar: "They both are pets and have four legs."
   Different: "The dog barks, and the cat meows."

2. *Sock* and *Shoe*
   Similar: "They both go on the feet."
   Different: "The sock is cloth, and the shoe is leather."

You could give some variety to this exercise when your reader is ready. You can give the difference and similarity and the category and have your reader name the objects. This works like this example on the next page:

"The category is clothing."
Similar: They both cover one end of a person.
Different: One is worn on the head, and the other is worn on the feet.

"Hat and *Shoes*."

ESTABLISHING ORDER

It's important for a reader to understand the order of events in a narration. It seems second nature to us, but it's sometimes not at all clear to a new reader that when a sentence has *after* in it, the event talked about is established in some time frame.

You're to write/speak a sentence which establishes time order (using words like: *then, when, next, after, while, during, before*) and your reader is to describe when the event takes place. It works like this:

While the boat burned, we swam to shore.

"When did the people swim to shore?"
"While the boat was burning."

We went home after we'd eaten dinner.

"When did they leave?"
"After they'd eaten."

IDENTIFYING CATEGORIES

We categorize constantly and automatically when we function in our adult lives, but we had to learn to do this. If a person were not to have this skill, each new object he'd come across would be in its own category and soon there would be too many categories to keep track. You can help your young reader learn this skill.

You're to list five or six words, and your reader is to tell you which word is not like the others or is in a different category. To do this your reader will have to place the words in an appropriate category, and the one that doesn't fit will be the one identified. This can be done orally or you can write out the listings. It could look like this listing:

skate
car
ball
bike
wagon
bus

Your reader will have to recognize a category that five of these objects will fit into and then will have to understand that the sixth one doesn't fit and will have to identify that category. In this case the category could be means of transportation. Your reader might say it like this:

"They all are ways to get somewhere except the *ball*, and that's a toy."

You'll have to be careful with this. It could go this way:

"They are all the same. They all roll on the ground, so they are all in the same category."

Boy, these kids!

MEANING

To the very young beginning reader any word seems like it must mean a specific thing, but we know that most words have a variety of meanings, depending on how and in what context they're used. It will help your reader if you work together, and three or four times a week, you list all of the meanings you can think of and find for a word. If you were to do this, it wouldn't take long before your student had a much better understanding of the complexity to be found in word meanings and had a much expanded vocabulary.

I still do this even after reading three to four books a week for thirty years. I find new meanings and shades of meaning to many words I thought I knew well. A good dictionary and an encyclopedia will help.

As an example or model for this exercise, let's examine the word *plate*. To a young child it might have just one meaning; it's what we eat our food from, and sometimes, when we go on a picnic, the plate is paper. This exercise will force you both to examine the meanings of words.

A plate can mean many things: *clutch plate*, as in a car; *collection plate*, as in church; *book plate* as in publishing; *page plate,* as in printing; *gold* or *silver plate*, as in jewelry; *electroplate*, as in manufacturing; *home plate*, as in baseball; *blue plate special,* as in a diner; *platefull,* as in being very busy; *what's on the plate*, as in a business meeting; *a plate,* as in a whole course of food at dinner; *plate,* as a horizontal timber laid on a foundation to receive the wall; *plate of beef,* as in a thin slice of brisket; *plating,* as in paper making to give high gloss; *plate,* as in any sheet of metal. Wow! Such a variety of meanings has to give any young reader an expanded image of the meaning of this word.

Now it may make more sense to you to think about reading as an act of interpretation. We understand when we read, as will your young reader, in relationship to what is brought to the page. If a child's understanding of the word *plate* is limited to that from which we eat our food, then much of the meaning in some writing may be lost.

When you first begin this exercise, you will have to be directive (decide what words to examine and how this is to be done), but soon your reader will want to help you select words. This can turn out to be a word treasure hunt. Have fun with it. I still do.

PART/WHOLE RELATIONSHIP

Your student will have to understand the relationships that words have, describe, or establish. Some words describe a part of another word which describes an object. You should have fun working on this exercise.

The point is to give your reader practice understanding the relationships between parts and wholes. You give the two words, and your reader tells you their relationship.

1. *motor—car*
   A motor is part of a car, so this relationship is part to whole.

2. *car—bus*
   A car is a whole and a bus is a whole, so this relationship is whole to whole.

3. *motor—tire*
   A motor is a part of a car and a tire is part of a car, so this relationship is part to part.

This can get confusing, and you should not let your reader get stuck in details unless that is fun. For instance, *piston* is part and *motor* is whole, so that in some situations, *motor* is part and in others it's whole.

To do this exercise you have to name only the objects or their relationships, and your reader can complete the exercise by naming either the relationships or the objects. Of course, if you were to name the relationships and were to ask your reader to name the objects, you would have to name a category for the objects. This would work like this: "I'll name a category and you, Johnny, will name the objects. Remember, I have to tell you if the relationship is part to part, whole to whole or part to whole. You'll have to tell me the names of two objects that have that relationship."

   "The category for this first game is *car* and the relationship is part to part. What are the objects?"
   "*Motor* and *tire*." (This could have been any two parts.)
   "Good for you. Now I'll name two objects and you're to tell me the relationship. *Pan* and *kettle*."
   "Whole to whole."
   "How about *pan* and *lid*?"
   "Whole to part."
   "Right! and what if the category is animal and the relationship is whole to whole?"
   "*Cat* and *chicken*."

72

If your young reader doesn't understand the rules for this game/exercise, wait for six months, and try again. It's better to wait a bit than to frustrate. Keep in mind that this has to be fun.

RECOGNIZING RELATED WORDS

Words are related in different ways. They may have similar characteristics, like a *rake* and a *shovel*—they both have long handles. They may be used for similar jobs, like a *comb* and a *brush*. They might be associated because of what they represent, like *cooking* and *dinner*.

You're to make a list of words followed by four or five other words, and your young reader is to tell you which of the following words is in some way related to the first word. This looks like this:

1. car — swing, football, bus, table, dog
2. nest — ticket, bed, dinner, home, hammer
3. bird — snow, feet, worm, horse, phone

If in number two your reader were to say *nest* is like *bed*, then your reader has created a category that includes both *bed* and *nest*. For baby birds and children, this is a logical category. If your reader were to make the category to include all birds and all people, then *nest* and *home* would be in the same category. You must not be too quick in judgment, for that could stifle creative thinking. If there is any logic at all to the categorization, then that is the kind of thinking about words you're trying to promote.

SYNONYMS

Another way to teach meaning is to have your young reader identify whether objects have similar meanings or if the meanings are different. You are to list orally or on paper a group of objects, and your young reader is to identify whether they are similar or not. This works like this:

"Johnny, I'm going to give you two words. You're to tell me if the words mean the same thing to you or not. Remember, there is no way you can be wrong in this because I asked you to tell me what they mean to you. If you tell me what they mean to you, you have to be right."
"Here we go. *Close* and *near.*"
"They're the same."
"Good. How about *apple* and *peach?*"
"They're the same and different."
"How could that be?"
"They're both fruit but different kinds."
"Okay, good for you. *Couple* and *pair.*"
"The same, but there might be a problem with that answer."
"How?"

"Pair to me means that the two things are related, like a *pair of shoes* or a *pair of socks*. In this case the two shoes or socks belong together. But *couple* could be two things that have no relationship at all. Like a couple of kids went swimming. But, sometimes a man and wife are called a couple, and they're related."

"Such excellent thinking on your part! *Money* and *pay?"*

"They're different, but not always."

"What?"

"Dad talks about getting his pay and that's the same as money."

You can see the reader thinking here. With some practice you both can learn a good deal about the relationships that some words can have.

SYNTAX

Now it gets complicated for the young reader. Words mean different things when they are in combination with other words. The combination brings to mind images (connotations) that are different for different people. Even though there are general (cultural) connotations for words, each of us has developed our own particular and personal connotations dependent upon our experiences, and these feelings about words, when they are influenced by the context of their use, give us our various understandings about what authors have in mind.

To help you understand how words in combination with other words take on different meanings, examine with me the words *old man*. Think of the situations and the ways to describe an old man, giving these two words very different connotations and thus giving us different feelings about them.

There is the description of grandpa as a *nice old man*. There is *old man Christmas*. There is the *dirty old man*. There is *old man time*. *Death* sometimes is referred as *the old man*. A tennis player at twenty-six is often considered an old man. A boxer is an old man at thirty. In the 1960's a man over thirty was considered to be an old man. There are kind, nasty, bearded, tired, lonely, homeless old men. Each of these bring to mind experiences we have had with the concept. The words that surround *old man* dictate how we feel about the old man in question and give different meanings to different people.

To help your student with this concept you might create a situation and then describe it so it establishes the meaning for the agreed upon words. To use words like *old man* you might create the situation (surrounding words) and have your student describe what the words *old man* in that situation mean. Your student will want to change roles with you in this exercise.

Another example that might help is the two words *near* and *far*. In understanding what these words mean it's important to know their syntactic situations. Think of how confusing the following could be to a young reader. The kitten crawled *far* from its mother. The moon is *near* Earth. It's *far* to the sun. All of the stars in our galaxy are *near* each other. It's too *far* to ride your bike to the store. The store is too *near* for Dad to take the car. Germany is *far* from here. Summer is *near*.

WORD ORDER

The order of words in an English sentence creates some of the meaning of the sentence. If the order of some words is changed, or even only the placement of one word, the meaning of the sentence changes. It will help your reader to get meaning from sentences if you do this exercise. You write/speak a sentence and have your reader change the placement of the words. See how many different ways the words can be put in the sentence and still have it make sense. This works this way:

After dinner the spider ate the small fly.

1. After the spider dinner, the small fly ate.
2. The spider ate dinner after the small fly.
3. After the dinner, Small, the fly, ate Spider. (cheat?)
4. The spider ate the small fly after dinner.
5. The fly dinner the small spider ate after. (It makes sense to me)
6. The spider ate after the small fly dinner.
7. The dinner ate spider after the small fly. (Not even me!)

Another exercise having to do with order is one where only one word is changed. The following example makes this clear.

You create the sentence and your reader changes the order of the one word as many times as is possible but still must make sense with the sentence:

Only John went to the store.
John *only* went to the store.
John went *only* to the store.
John went to the *only* store.
John went to the store *only*. (Weak, but okay.)
John went to *only* the store. (I don't talk this way.)

APPENDIX

TEACHING LITERATURE THE SOCRATIC WAY

The following six stories, of increasing sophistication, are followed by examples of Socratic dialogue. They're not presented for you to use with your children; rather, they are given only as examples and were chosen because I felt that most parents would be familiar with them.

HORTENSE AND FREDDY
a
STICKY ROMANCE

Hortense knew she was beautiful. In fact, she was so pleased at how good looking she was, she spent most of her days gazing at her reflection in the surface of the pond where she lived.

If there was even a speck of dirt on her slick, green body, she would flick it off with her long and sticky tongue.

One day, after cleaning herself until she almost sparkled in the morning sun, she found her tongue was no longer sticky. She had worn all the sticky off! When she flicked out her tongue to catch food, the bugs bounced off its tip. Dragonflies perched on her head, and spiders sat in the shade she made on her lily pad and ignored her.

Surrounded by food, Hortense was starving. She grew thin and began to lose her beauty. Now, when she slowly flicked her tongue against her dull skin, the dirt would smear, and she spent much of her time silently weeping.

Hortense feared she would die if she couldn't catch flies, and she couldn't if she had no sticky on her tongue. She sat on her lily pad and cried, "Oh, what a beautiful but sad thing I am. I will starve and be lost to the world."

Freddy heard her sighing this way. He was large and very ugly, but he loved Hortense more than anything in his world. He swam to Hortense's lily pad and gazed at his beautiful dreamfrog. Hortense had pressed the back of her thin and very pale hand against her brow.

She jerked her hand down when she saw him and said, in an angry but very weak voice, "Go away, Freddy. You know I am too beautiful to pay any attention to you."

Freddy tried to smile through the pain he felt for Hortense and whispered up at her, "I heard you crying. Is there anything I can do to help?"

Hortense took a long breath and said, "No. I will just have to starve because I have lost the sticky on my tongue." Freddy was smart, but this was a very serious problem. Thinking as hard as he ever had, he drifted to the bottom of the pond.

Freddy stayed in the mud at the bottom for a long time and rose to the surface only after he had thought of a way to save his beautiful Hortense.

On the bank near their pond, Freddy found a small field of flowers. When he stuck his tongue into the center of a blossom, the pollen made it so sticky that catching a fly was one of the easiest things he had ever done.

Freddy swam quickly out to his lovely Hortense, and, holding onto the edge of her lily pad and gazing up into her sad face said, "Hortense, I love you. If I tell you how to get your tongue sticky again, will you be my girlfrog?"

Hortense was still for so long Freddy began to think she had not heard him. The still beautiful but very lean Hortense turned slowly and looked down at Freddy over her narrow and thinning nose.

It was after a long discussion and many agreements reached that Freddy and Hortense swam toward the bank and the field of blue blossoms.

Today, if you were to go to that same pond, you might see beautiful small frogs who slide the tips of their tongues into the center of flowers.

And, if you had time to wait and were very lucky, you might see larger, and not-so-pretty frogs who spend long periods of time lying in the mud at the bottom of the pond, thinking.

Teacher:	Okay, it's your turn now. What was the point of that story?
Reader:	I think there was a message, or what you call a moral.
Teacher:	A story with one is often called a fable. Sometimes this kind of a story is an allegory if figurative language is used. For instance frogs are personified. That means that they are presented as having human characteristics.
Reader:	They sure did in that story. I forgot that they were frogs and started thinking they were people. They think just like people do. What do you suppose frogs think about?
Teacher:	Would you believe me if I told you?
Reader:	I don't think so.
Teacher:	Let's call that story a fable. This means it has a moral. What is it?
Reader:	I think there were two. One was that if you love yourself enough it gets expensive, and you have to pay for it.
Teacher:	Good. Support that.
Reader:	What do you mean, support it?
Teacher:	Tell me where in the text you got that idea. How does the story support your statement?
Reader:	Hortense loves herself so much that she keeps cleaning her body with her tongue and the sticky wears off. Is that possible?
Teacher:	No. Okay, so she has to pay for her love of herself. Is that a reasonable moral to pass on in a story?
Reader:	Sure. You always told me that there's no such thing as a free lunch. We have to pay for everything we get in one way or another.
Teacher:	Is that a moral?
Reader:	What's a moral? Can you give me a definition?
Teacher:	It's an identification of something that is right or wrong. It's like a rule to live by. A thing is good or bad. If it's good it's moral, and if it's bad it's immoral.
Reader:	Is that a thing or a rule or an attitude?

Teacher:	It can be anything that you call a good thing. Is the rule that you shouldn't love yourself too much a good thing?
Reader:	In this story it is.
Teacher:	Good for you. That's the point of a fable, to show the reader what's good. You said that there were two morals in this story. What's the second one?
Reader:	Most problems can be solved if a person works at them hard enough.
Teacher:	Do you think that's true?
Reader:	I don't know. It's what the story says, but I never thought much about it. I always figured you'd solve problems for me.
Teacher:	Your turn will come. I can tell you what I think is moral, but I can't force you to accept what I say. You'll have to come to your own decisions about what's good.
Reader:	But there are lots of rules about what's good. There are laws about what's bad. There are lots of rules in church about what's good. In clubs like Campfire Girls and Cub Scouts there are rules about what's good. There is even the "Pledge of Allegiance" and the "Declaration of Independence." They both tell what's good.
Teacher:	That's true. They have rules to live by. But you have to adopt those rules as your own. You have to say to yourself, "I believe in so and so," then you can make the hard decisions in life.
Reader:	We're a long way from the story, aren't we?
Teacher:	Not really. This is what a fable is supposed to do, make you think about what is the right thing to do. It's a way of teaching morals.
Reader:	There is one other lesson in the story.
Teacher:	What's that?
Reader:	If you have a really serious problem, you can solve it best from under water.
Teacher:	If I had a bucket of water here I could solve lots of problems.

she leapt as lightly as a squirrel among the branches, and the Prince did not know what had become of her. So he waited until the father came, and then he told him that the strange maiden had rushed from him, and that he thought she had gone up into the pear tree.

The father thought to himself, "It surely cannot be Cinderella," and called for an axe, and felled the tree, but there was no one in it. And when they went into the kitchen there sat Cinderella among the cinders, as usual, for she had got down the other side of the tree, and had taken back her beautiful clothes to the bird on the hazel bush, and had put on her old gray kirtle again.

On the third day, when the parents and the step-sisters had set off, Cinderella went again to her mother's grave, and said to the tree,

"Little tree, little tree, shake over me,
That silver and gold may come down and cover me."

Then the bird cast down a dress, the like of which had never been seen for splendor and brilliancy, and slippers that were of gold.

And when she appeared in this dress at the feast, nobody knew what to say for wonderment. The Prince danced with her alone, and if any one else asked her he answered, "She is my partner."

And when it was evening Cinderella wanted to go home, and the Prince was about to go with her, when she ran past him so quickly that he could not follow her. But he had laid a plan, and had caused all the steps to be spread with pitch, so that as she rushed down them the left shoe of the maiden remained sticking in it. The Prince picked it up, and saw that it was of gold, and very small and slender. The next morning he went to the father and told him that none should be his bride save the one whose foot the golden shoe should fit.

Then the two sisters were very glad, because they had pretty feet. The eldest went to her room to try on the shoe, and her mother stood by. But she could not get her great toe into it, for the shoe was too small. Then her mother said, "Put some soap on your foot to make it slippery and jump up and down on that foot to force it into the shoe," which the daughter did. Then with her foot bulging from the small shoe she went down to the Prince. Then he took her with him on his horse as his bride, and rode off. They had to pass by the grave, and there sat the two pigeons on the hazel bush, and they cried,

"There they go, there they go!
There is blood on her shoe;
The shoe is too small,
Not the right bride at all!"

Then the Prince looked at her shoe, and saw the blood. And he turned his horse round and took the false bride home again, saying she was not the right one, and that the other sister must try on the shoe. So she went into her room to do so, but her foot was so small that the shoe flopped off each time she took a step. Her mother said, "Stuff some old rags into the toe to keep the shoe on and the daughter did and went down to the Prince, who took his bride before him on his horse and rode off. When they passed by the hazel bush the two pigeons sat there and cried,

The following story, "Cinderella," is a good one to use to show the various methods of analyzing fiction. The version of this favorite story given here is the classic one with some slight editing. Some of the phraseology and punctuation may seem strange, for it's a translation from the German, first printed in 1812.

CINDERELLA

There was once a rich man whose wife lay sick, and when she felt her end drawing near she called to her only daughter to come near her bed, and said, "Dear child, be good and pious, and God will always take care of you, and I will look down upon you from heaven and will be with you."

And then she closed her eyes and died. The maiden went every day to her mother's grave and wept, and was always pious and good. When the winter came the snow covered the grave with a white covering, and when the sun came in the early spring and melted it away, the man took to himself another wife.

The new wife brought two daughters home with her, and they were beautiful and fair in appearance, but at heart were ugly. And then began very evil times for the poor step-daughter.

"Is the stupid creature to sit in the same room with us?" said they. "Those who eat food must earn it. She is nothing but a kitchen-maid."

They took away her pretty dresses and put on her an old gray kirtle and gave her wooden shoes to wear.

"Just look now at the proud princess, how she is decked out!" cried they laughing, and then they sent her into the kitchen. There she was obliged to do heavy work from morning to night, get up early in the morning, draw water, make the fires, cook, and wash. Besides that, the sisters did their utmost to torment her—mocking her, and strewing peas and lentils among the ashes, and setting her to pick them up. In the evenings, when she was quite tired out with her hard day's work, she had no bed to lie on, but was obliged to rest on the hearth among the cinders. And because she always looked dusty and dirty, as if she had slept in the cinders, they named her Cinderella.

It happened one day that the father went to the fair, and he asked his two step-daughters what he should bring back for them. "Fine clothes!" said one. "Pearls and jewels!" said the other.

"But what will you have, Cinderella?" said he.

"The first twig, father, that strikes against your hat on the way home; that is what I should like you to bring me."

So he brought for the two step-daughters fine clothes, pearls, and jewels, and on his way back, as he rode through a green lane, a hazel twig struck against his hat. He broke it off and carried it home with him. And when he reached home he gave to the step-daughters what they had wished for, and to Cinderella he gave the hazel twig. She thanked him and went to her mother's grave and planted this twig there, weeping so bitterly that the tears fell upon it and watered it, and it flourished and became a fine tree. Cinderella went to see it three times a day, and wept and prayed, and each time a white bird rose up from the tree, and if she uttered any wish the bird brought her whatever she had wished for.

Now it came to pass that the King ordained a festival that should last for three days, and to which all the beautiful young women of that country were bidden, so that the King's son might choose a bride from among them. When the two step-daughters heard that they too were bidden to appear, they felt very pleased, and they called Cinderella and said, "Comb our hair, brush our shoes, and make our buckles fast, we are going to the wedding feast at the King's castle."

When she heard this, Cinderella could not help crying, for she too would have liked to go to the dance, and she begged her step-mother to allow her. "What! You Cinderella!" said she, "In all your dust and dirt, you want to go to the festival? You that have no dress and no shoes, you want to dance?"

But as she persisted in asking, at last the step-mother said, "I have stewed a dishful of lentils in the ashes, and if you can pick them all up again in two hours you may go with us."

Then the maiden went to the back door that led into the garden and called out,

"O gentle doves, O turtle-doves,
And all the birds that be,
The lentils that in ashes lie
Come and pick up for me!
The good must be put in the dish,
The bad you may eat if you wish."

Then there came to the kitchen window two white doves, and after them some turtle-doves, and at last a crowd of all the birds under heaven, chirping and fluttering, and they alighted among the ashes. The doves nodded with their heads and began to pick, peck, pick, peck, and then all the others began to pick, peck, pick, peck, and put all the good grains into the dish. Before an hour was over all was done, and they flew away.

Then the maiden brought the dish to her step-mother, feeling joyful, and thinking that now she should go to the feast, but the step-mother said, "No, Cinderella, you have no proper clothes, and you do not know how to dance, and you would be laughed at!" And when Cinderella cried for disappointment, she added, "If you can pick two dishes full of lentils out of the ashes, you shall go with us," thinking to herself, "for that is not possible."

When she had strewed two dishes full of lentils among the ashes the maiden went through the back door into the garden, and cried,

"O gentle doves, O turtle-doves,
And all the birds that be,
The lentils that in ashes lie
Come and pick up for me!
The good must be put in the dish,
The bad you may eat if you wish."

So there came to the kitchen window two white doves, and then some turtle-doves, and at last a crowd of all the other birds, chirping and fluttering, and they alighted among the ashes, and the doves nodded with their heads and began to pick, peck, pick, peck, and then

all the others began to pick, peck, pick, peck, and put all the good grains into the dish. And before half-an-hour was over it was all done, and they flew away. Then the maiden took the dishes to the step-mother, feeling joyful, and thinking that now she should go with them to the feast, but she said, "All this is of no good; you cannot come with us for you have no proper clothes and cannot dance; you would put us to shame." Then she turned her back on poor Cinderella and made haste to set out with her two proud daughters.

And as there was no one left in the house, Cinderella went to her mother's grave, under the hazel bush, and cried,

"Little tree, little tree, shake over me,
That silver and gold may come down and cover me."

Then the bird threw down a dress of gold and silver, and a pair of slippers embroidered with silk and silver. And in all haste she put on the dress and went to the festival. But her step-mother and step-sisters did not know her, and thought she must be a foreign Princess, she looked so beautiful in her golden dress. Of Cinderella they never thought at all, and supposed that she was sitting at home, and picking the lentils out of the ashes. The King's son came to meet her, and took her by the hand and danced with her, and he refused to stand up with anyone else, so that he might not be obliged to let go her hand, and when any one came to claim it he answered, "She is my partner."

And when the evening came she wanted to go home, but the Prince said he would go with her to take care of her, for he wanted to see where the beautiful maiden lived. But she escaped him, and jumped up into the pigeon-house. Then the Prince waited until the father came, and told him the strange maiden had jumped into the pigeon-house. The father thought to himself, "It surely cannot be Cinderella," and called for axes and hatchets, and had the pigeon-house cut down, but there was no one in it. And when they entered the house there sat Cinderella in her dirty clothes among the cinders, and a little oil lamp burnt dimly in the chimney. Cinderella had been very quick, and had jumped out of the pigeon house again, and had run to the hazel bush, and there she had taken off her beautiful dress and had laid it on the grave, and the bird had carried it away again, and then she had put on her little gray kirtle again, and had sat down in the kitchen among the cinders. The next day, when the festival began anew, and the parents and step-sisters had gone to it, Cinderella went to the hazel bush and cried,

"Little tree, little tree, shake over me,
That silver and gold may come down and cover me."

Then the bird cast down a still more splendid dress than on the day before. And when she appeared in it among the guests, everyone was astonished at her beauty. The Prince had been waiting until she came, and he took her hand and danced with her alone. And when any one else came to invite her he said, "She is my partner."

And when the evening came she wanted to go home, and the Prince followed her, for he wanted to see to what house she belonged; but she broke away from him, and ran into the garden at the back of the house. There stood a fine large tree, bearing splendid pears;

"There they go, there they go!
The shoe is falling off;
Her foot is too small,
Not the right bride at all!"

Then the Prince looked at her foot, and saw how the shoe was hanging from her toe, and he turned his horse round and brought the false bride home again. "This is not the right one," said he, "have you no other daughter?"

"No," said the man, "only my dead wife left behind her a little stunted Cinderella; it is impossible that she can be the bride." But the King's son ordered her to be sent for, but the mother said, "Oh no! she is much too dirty, I could not let her be seen," but he would have her fetched, and so Cinderella had to appear.

First she washed her face and hands quite clean, and went in and curtsied to the Prince, who held out to her the golden shoe. Then she sat down on a stool, drew her foot out of the heavy wooden shoe, and slipped it into the golden one, which fitted it perfectly. And when she stood up, and the Prince looked in her face, he knew again the beautiful maiden that had danced with him, and he cried, "This is the right bride!" The step-mother and the two sisters were thunderstruck, and grew pale with anger; but he put Cinderella before him on his horse and rode off. And as they passed the hazel bush, the two white pigeons cried,

"There they go, there they go!
The shoe's not too big;
Her foot's not too small,
The right bride is she after all."

And when they had thus cried, they came flying after and perched on Cinderella's shoulders, one on the right, the other on the left, and so remained.

And when her wedding with the Prince was appointed to be held, the false sisters came, hoping to curry favor and to take part in the festivities. So as the bridal procession went to the church, the eldest walked on the right side and the younger walked on the left, but both were limping badly, which they both did for the rest of their days because of their wickedness and falsehood.

The suggested methods of helping your reader understand stories can be applied to almost any story, and "Cinderella" is used here as an example of how they may work. There has been some editing here, because the version of these tales as they appeared in the original translation are fairly strong and brutal. Because of the detail of these observations and the complexity of the ideas, this level of interpretation is designed for readers who are between the ages of nine and twelve. A careful reading of this story will produce understanding of motivation if an examination is made of the list on the next page:

I. CHARACTERS' ACTIONS:

A. **Cinderella:** (What she says and does—and does not do):

1.   ". . .went to her mother's grave every day and wept."
2.   "She was always pious and good."
3.   She wears what the sisters give her and says nothing to her father about it.
4.   She has to do heavy kitchen work all day.
5.   She has to sleep in the cinders. She doesn't complain.
6.   She asks only for a twig from the fair.
7.   She is polite for she thanks her father for the twig.
8.   She plants the twig at her mother's grave and weeps.
9.   She visits the grave and tree three times a day and prays.
10.   She begs her step-mother to let her go to the dance.
11.   "She persisted in asking." She teases her step-mother.
12.   She asks the birds two times to help her pick up the seeds.
13.   She asks the tree three times to give her silver and gold clothes.
14.   She goes to the dance three times, even though she has been told that she can't go by her step-mother.
15.   On three nights she dances with the Prince, runs away from him, hides, and changes into her old clothes to fool her father and the Prince.
16.   She doesn't ask the tree to mend her sisters' feet so that they'll not have to limp for the rest of their days.
17.   She doesn't ask the tree to make her life easier or to make her step-mother and step-sisters more pleasant.

B. **Cinderella's father:**

1.   He doesn't go to the grave with Cinderella or even visit it on his own.
2.   He marries again within a few months.
3.   He marries a woman who has two daughters and doesn't discuss this with Cinderella.
4.   He doesn't interfere with the step-mother's and her daughters' abuse of Cinderella (his own daughter).
5.   He lets Cinderella sleep in the ashes.
6.   He lets the step-sisters take Cinderella's nice clothes.
7.   He brings his step-daughters fine clothes and jewels and brings only a twig for his daughter.
8.   He goes to the festival with his new wife and daughters but leaves Cinderella home alone.
9.   He doesn't invite Cinderella to go to the festival.
10.   He calls his own daughter ". . .a little stunted Cinderella."
11.   He doesn't even consider that Cinderella could be the beautiful girl the Prince is looking for.

C. The Step-sisters:

1. They take Cinderella's pretty dresses and put her in an old gray kirtle and give her wooden shoes to wear.
2. "`Just look at the proud princess, how she is decked out!' cried they laughing."
3. They make Cinderella do heavy work from morning to night, get up early in the morning, draw water, make the fires, cook and wash.
4. They do their utmost to torment her—mocking her, and strewing peas and lentils among the ashes, and setting her to pick them up.
5. They name her Cinderella.
6. They ask their father to bring them from the fair fine clothes and pearls and jewels.
7. They are pleased that they have been bidden to appear at the festival.
8. They tell Cinderella, "Comb our hair, brush our shoes, and make our buckles fast, we are going to the wedding feast at the King's castle."
9. They are glad that the bride should be the one the golden shoe should fit for they have pretty feet.
10. They both hurt their feet with the shoe.
11. They hope to curry favor at the wedding.
12. They are part of the wedding and limp next to Cinderella.
13. They are lame for the rest of their lives.

D. The Step-mother:

1. Marries the father soon after the death of Cinderella's mother.
2. Brings two daughters to live with Cinderella and her father.
3. Doesn't try to make friends with Cinderella.
4. Allows the sisters to abuse Cinderella
5. Lets Cinderella do the heavy work alone.
6. Allows/encourages the father to give special treatment to her two daughters.
7. Will not allow Cinderella to go to the festival.
8. Says, "What! you Cinderella, in all your dust and dirt, you want to go to the festival! you that have no dress and no shoes! you want to dance!"
9. She throws lentils in the ashes and says, "If you can pick them all up again in two hours you may go with us."
10. When Cinderella brings the dish full she says, "No, Cinderella, you have no proper clothes, and you do not know how to dance, and you would be laughed at!"
11. She tells Cinderella that if she can pick two dishes full she can go to the festival.
12. When Cinderella comes to her with two dishes full she says, "All this is of no good to you; you cannot come with us, for you have no proper clothes, and cannot dance; you would put us to shame."
13. She leaves with her two daughters for the festival.
14. She tells her daughter to force her foot into the shoe.
15. She tells the other daughter to stuff rags into the shoe so it will fit.

16. When the Prince asks to meet Cinderella she says, "Oh no! she is much too dirty, I could not let her be seen."
17. She grows pale with anger when Cinderella is able to fit the shoe.

E. **The Prince:**

1. He dances with Cinderella.
2. He'll stand with no one else.
3. He says, "She is my partner."
4. He wants to go home with Cinderella and take care of her.
5. He lets Cinderella get away from him by jumping into the pigeon-house and a tree in the garden.
6. He tells the father that a strange maiden has rushed from him.
7. He puts pitch on the steps to catch her shoe.
8. He tells his father that none should be the bride but the one whose foot the shoe should fit.
9. He decides to find by shoe size the girl with whom he has danced for three nights and fallen in love.
10. He tries the shoe on the two sisters.
11. He rides off with the two sisters until he sees that the shoe doesn't fit them.
12. He doesn't recognize that they are not the one he had been dancing with for three nights.
13. He doesn't try to recognize his bride-to-be by any other means, such as by her appearance.
14. When Cinderella puts on the shoe, he cries, "This is the right bride!"

Now that we have a listing of the actions of the characters, we should be able to come to some conclusions about the author's intent in this story. Let's have a dialogue with a young reader who is about thirteen years old:

Teacher: That sure is a happy ending. . .or is it?
Reader: What do you mean, ". . .or is it?"
Teacher: Cinderella gets to marry the prince. That's what the story is about isn't it?
Reader: I don't know if I'm sure what the conflict is. Can we talk about that?
Teacher: What are the relationships of the characters in this story?
Reader: Cinderella's mother's dead. Her father, her step-mother and her two step-sisters all seem to be against her. They like each other.
Teacher: Who else is there?
Reader: The Prince. But we don't know anything about him at all except he's not too bright.
Teacher: Any other force?
Reader: What do you mean?
Teacher: Are there any other things at work here for her?
Reader: Like the birds?
Teacher: Sure, what of them?

Reader: They're working for Cinderella. They come from her mother who is in heaven. That's a force for good. They help with the lentils and the clothes and they warn the Prince when he has the wrong bride.

Teacher: Who do we know the most about?

Reader: Cinderella, of course. We know lots about her.

Teacher: Okay, what do we know about Cinderella?

Reader: We know she's good and pious, but she lets people take advantage of her and doesn't say anything about it. She loves her mother. She's willing to do all the hard work and let the others rest. She talks to birds. She works hard to go to the dance, then when she gets a chance to be with the Prince, she runs away and hides. She doesn't tell people that she's the one who the shoe fits.

Teacher: That's a lot. What kind of a person is she?

Reader: Innocent and stupid.

Teacher: That's kind of harsh, isn't it?

Reader: That's what she is.

Teacher: Okay, and what about the rest of them?

Reader: Stupid, at least the Prince is, lazy, selfish, thoughtless, cruel and greedy.

Teacher: Not a nice bunch of people.

Reader: That must be who the antagonists are. Everybody else.

Teacher: You think that Cinderella is the protagonist and everybody else is against her?

Reader: The Prince isn't against her, but he's so dumb that he might as well be.

Teacher: What do we have for a conflict here then?

Reader: Cinderella is innocent and good.

Teacher: What about the other side?

Reader: They're dumb and bad.

Teacher: Let's label the conflict then.

Reader: Innocence and goodness against stupidity and greed.

Teacher: Wow, that's a mouthful. But, what of the birds?

Reader: The birds are on Cinderella's side just like her mother is. The birds are innocent and good. Doesn't it look that way to you?

Teacher: The way you put it sounds good to me. I didn't think of the story that way until now, but I think you've done some good thinking here, and I agree it looks the way you describe it.

Reader: Good.

Teacher: I've got one more question. You keep calling the Prince stupid. Why?

Reader: Because of the way he acts. The author must want us to think that he's really dumb.

Teacher: You'll have to explain that.

Reader: Okay. The Prince wants to get married, so he has a dance for all the girls in the land, and they come to his party, and he dances only with Cinderella. He's with her for three nights, maybe six or seven hours a night. Facing her, talking to her, holding her hand and dancing with her. Then when he wants to find her again, the only way he can think to do it is by her shoe size. He's got to be stupid.

Teacher: I'm convinced. The Prince is stupid. He even chooses the wrong girl based on her shoe size—twice! The birds have to tell him he's got the wrong ones.

The very old but classic story, "Rumpelstiltskin," looks to be quite simple but is deceptive. We'll never know if this is intentional on the writer's part or not. You'll have to decide for yourself just as do Teacher and Reader in the following conversation.

You'll recognize the techniques listed earlier as methods used to understand literature when they are employed here by both Teacher and Reader. Notice that Reader is improving in the ability to understand stories and in talking about them with Teacher.

RUMPELSTILTSKIN

There was once a miller who was poor, but he had one beautiful daughter. It happened one day that he came to speak with the King, and to give himself consequence, he told him that he had a daughter who could spin gold out of straw. The King said to the miller, "That is an art that pleases me well; if your daughter is as cleaver as you say, bring her to my castle tomorrow, that I may put her to the proof."

When the girl was brought to him, he led her into a room that was quite full of straw, and gave her a wheel and spindle, and said, "Now set to work, and if by the early morning you have not spun this straw to gold you shall die." And he shut the door himself, and left her there alone.

And so the poor miller's daughter was left there sitting, and could not think what to do for her life: she had no notion how to set to work to spin gold from straw, and her distress grew so great that she began to weep. Then all at once the door opened, and in came a little man, who said, "Good evening, miller's daughter; why are you crying?"

"Oh," answered the girl, "I have got to spin gold out of straw, and I don't understand the business."

Then the little man said, "What will you give me if I spin it for you?"

"My necklace," said the girl.

The little man took the necklace, seated himself before the wheel, and whir, whir, whir! three times round and the bobbin was full; then he took up another, whir whir, whir! three times round, then that one was full; and so he went on till the morning, when all the straw had been spun, and all the bobbins were full of gold. At sunrise came the King, and when he saw the gold he was astonished and very much rejoiced, for he was very avaricious. He had the miller's daughter taken into another room filled with straw, much bigger than the last, and he told her that as she valued her life she must spin it all in one night.

The girl did not know what to do, so she began to cry, and then the door opened, and the little man appeared and said, "What will you give me if I spin all this straw into gold?"

"The ring from my finger," answered the girl.

So the little man took the ring, and began again to send the wheel whirring round, and by the next morning all the straw was spun into glistening gold. The King was rejoiced beyond measure at the sight, but as he could never have enough gold, he had the miller's daughter taken into a still larger room filled with straw, and said, "This too, must be spun in one night, and if you accomplish it you shall be my wife." For he thought, "Although she is but a miller's daughter, I am not likely to find anyone richer in the whole world."

As soon as the girl was left alone, the little man appeared for the third time and said, "What will you give me if I spin the straw for you this time?"

"I have nothing left to give," answered the girl.

"Then you must promise me the first child you have after you are Queen," said the little man.

"But who knows whether that will happen?" thought the girl; but as she did not know what else to do in her necessity, she promised the little man what he desired, upon which he began to spin, until all the straw was gold. And when in the morning the King came and found all done according to his wish, he caused the wedding to be held at once, and the miller's pretty daughter became a Queen.

In a year's time she brought a fine child into the world, and thought no more of the little man, but one day he came suddenly into her room, and said, "Now give me what you promised me."

The Queen was terrified greatly, and offered the little man all the riches of the kingdom if he would only leave the child; but the little man said, "No, I would rather have something living than all the treasures of the world."

Then the Queen began to lament and to weep, so that the little man had pity upon her. "I will give you three days," said he, "and if at the end of that time you cannot guess my name, you must give up the child to me."

Then the Queen spent the whole night in thinking over all the names that she had ever heard, and sent a messenger through the land to ask far and wide for all the names that could be found. And when the little man came the next day, beginning with Caspar, Melchior, Balthazar, she repeated all she knew, and went through the whole list, but after each the little man said, "That is not my name."

The third day the messenger came back again, and said, "I have not been able to find one single new name; but as I passed through the woods I came to a high hill, and near it was a little house, and before the house burned a fire, and round the fire danced a comical little man, and he hopped on one leg and cried,

"Today do I bake, tomorrow I brew
The day after that the Queen's child comes in;
And oh! I am glad that nobody knew
That the name I am called is Rumpelstiltskin!"

You cannot think how pleased the Queen was to hear the name, and soon afterwards, when the little man walked in and said, "Now, Mrs. Queen, what is my name?" she said at first, "Are you called Jack?"

"No," answered he.

"Are you called Harry?" she asked again.

"No," answered he.

And then she said, "Then perhaps your name is Rumplestiltskin!"

"You cheated me! You cheated me," cried the little man, and in his anger he stamped with his right foot so hard that it went into the ground above his knee; then he seized his left foot in such a fury that he broke himself in half, and there was an end of him.

Teacher: That story sure ends the way it should.

Reader: Why do you say that?

Teacher: The Queen gets to keep her baby. All the people are happy for the rest of their lives. This is the way stories are supposed to end, isn't it?

Reader: I didn't think there was a way that stories were supposed to end. I thought they just end the way they do and we have to accept how it happens.

Teacher: Of course, you're right. How do you think it ends?

Reader: I find it kind of sad.

Teacher: Sad! That's a funny thing to say. The Queen is happy, the baby gets to stay with its mother and the little man is out of her life. What more could you want?

Reader: Let's look at what happens here.

Teacher: That sounds like me.

Reader: It's supposed to. Now, let's examine the characters for motive and then try to figure out the forces in conflict. When we know those two things, we'll be able to decide if the ending is happy or not.

Teacher: Okay, you're doing fine. Start us off.

Reader: What does the girl want?

Teacher: The first night she just wants to stay alive.

Reader: What does she do to do that?

Teacher: She promises her necklace to the little man if he'll spin gold for her.

Reader: The second night?

Teacher: She promises her ring for the same thing.

Reader: How does this keep her alive?

Teacher: The King says he'll kill her if she can't spin straw into gold.

Reader: Not a very nice King. And the third night?

Teacher: She has no more jewelry to give the little man and she promises him her child.

Reader: Or the King will kill her?

Teacher: No. He'll marry her if she can spin gold the third night. Oh! That's not so good, is it? She gives up her child for the chance to become the wife of a man who would kill a girl if she couldn't spin gold out of straw. Greedy or thoughtless or stupid or something not so nice, isn't it?

Reader: Right. Not so nice. She makes a bargain with the little man three times. What happens when it comes to paying the man for the third roomful of gold?

Teacher: I see where you're going now. She doesn't want to pay him. She cries and carries on so badly that he gives her another chance to get out of the bargain.

Reader: What does he offer?

Teacher: That if she can know his name in three days she can keep her child.

Reader: No. That's not what the story says at all. Look at it. He says, "Guess my name." She makes another bargain to try to guess his name to keep her child.

Teacher: Good reading on your part. I missed that.

Reader: What happens then when the little man comes back the third day?

Teacher: She tells him his name, and he dies.

Reader: How does she guess his name?

Teacher: She doesn't guess it. She knows what it is because she is told what it is by her messenger.

Reader: How does he know?

Teacher: He tells her he spied on the little man and heard him singing a song with his name in it.

Reader: So, what are the actions of the girl? She takes part in the deception of the King about her ability to spin gold out of straw. She agrees to give up her baby for a chance to be Queen. She wants to marry a man willing to kill girls. She breaks her promise to the little man about giving him her child. She uses information from a person who spies on the little man to cheat him out of the bargain. In fact, she lies to the little man because she doesn't guess his name at all.

Teacher: What about the little man. He isn't so nice is he?

Reader: What he does is offer his services to the girl when she feels so sorry for herself. He keeps his side of the bargain. He spins gold out of straw for three nights. When he comes to collect, he feels so sorry for the girl that he gives her another chance to keep the child. He is cheated out of the child. He says, "I would rather have something living than all the treasures of the world." (Just the opposite of what the girl does: she agrees to give up a living thing for a social position.)

Teacher: That's a whole new way for me to look at this story. I always thought that the girl was the protagonist and the little old man was the antagonist. I sure read it backward.

Reader: If the girl is the protagonist, what does she want and what's keeping her from it?

Teacher: I see now. Nothing keeps her from being Queen once the little man helps her. If she's the protagonist, then there's no antagonist. Good for you!

You may not make the same interpretation as did Reader, but that's one of the wonderful things about reading. There are opportunities for different views. Another way to look at this story is that the girl is the protagonist and there are great forces against her getting what she wants, which is to stay alive and to keep her child. She is made to perform, in what must seem to her to be impossible ways, or she'll be killed. This by a king. She is only a miller's daughter. What an imbalance of forces at work. Then, as if by magic, a little man appears and can do the impossible. He can spin gold out of straw. Of course, she promises him anything he wants. She is in the grip of very powerful forces here.

When it comes time to give up her child, it's understandable that she doesn't wish to do so, since it is an agreement made under great stress and threat. She is willing to do anything, as would we all, to keep her child. A deception of a little man is a small price to pay to keep her only child. It's not her intent that the little man would die.

If we look at the story this way, we have the girl as the protagonist and the antagonist forces against her are her father's lying about her spinning, the king's greed, the threat against her life by the king, the little man's ability to spin gold and a last chance to save her child. Very unequal forces indeed to create suspense.

And yet another way to look at this story is to take the position that all of the characters are on the same protagonistic side. The antagonistic forces they battle are a combination of their own weaknesses and the structures of society and the supernatural forces in the universe/mind. The king wants wealth, something most people would like. The miller wants the favor of the king, a not unreasonable ambition. The daughter wants to stay alive, to be a queen and to save her child, all of which are not unnatural desires. The little man wants the companionship of a child; good for him. These people are helped or kept from their goals by the forces against them such as politics, natural laws, human greed and loneliness, political ambition above family needs (not an unusual situation even in American politics) and aspirations to social or financial positions (which is not unheard of or too widely frowned upon even today). This is an interesting and complicated story.

LITTLE RED RIDING HOOD

There once lived a girl called Little Red Riding Hood. She was very good about keeping house and even helped with the baking.

One morning Little Red Riding Hood told her mother that she wanted to visit her grandmother, but her mother told her that the old woman was ill. "All the more reason for a visit," cried Little Red. Her mother fixed her a basket of food and medicine for the sweet old lady and warned the little girl not to stop on the way through the forest, for there were strange and dangerous things that lived there.

On the way Red Riding Hood did stop to pick some flowers to put in her basket and saw a large wolf leaning against the bole of an ancient tree.

"Where are you going, little girl?" said the wolf.

"This is very strange," thought Little Red, "a talking wolf." She wasn't sure exactly what to think. She had been trained not to talk to strangers, but she had also been taught to be polite to all people. This was not a person. This was a wolf! What to do?

She decided to speak and see what would happen. "To visit my grandmother who is sick." Little Red felt silly for talking to a wolf and a bit scared, for she had heard stories about wolves!

"That is sad," said the wolf. "What do you have in that nice basket?" he asked, stepping closer and reaching to lift the cover.

"Some things for my grandmother," said Little Red. Then she realized that the wolf might take her grandmother's food and she added, even though it was a lie—she felt it was okay to lie if she were protecting her grandmother's food—"bug spray, floor polish and an old pair of shoes."

"Where does she live?" asked the wolf, losing interest in the basket.

"At the end of this path on the other side of the woods," said Little Red, beginning to walk away.

"Here, give her this flower," he said, handing Red Riding Hood a small blue flower.

The wolf then turned and ran off. He was hurrying to her grandmother's house before Little Red Riding Hood could get there! On the path he picked some flowers and put them on his head, trying to look like a little girl.

When he knocked on the door, he heard a faint voice call out, "Who's there?" In a high and small voice the wolf said, "It is I, Grandmother, Little Red Riding Hood. I have come with a basket of food from mother.

"Come in and kiss your grandmother."

And that's what the wolf did. He went in, but instead of kissing the old lady, he gobbled her up in one bite. He was so hungry he didn't even chew her but swallowed her whole!

He then looked out of the window toward the path from the woods. A sly smile played across his face as he quickly put on a nightgown and a nightcap he found in the cupboard. When he had pulled the nightcap down over his long ears, he got into the old lady's bed! What a strange thing to do.

When Little Red came into her grandmother's house, there was her grandmother all covered up with blankets, with just her nightcap and her nose showing. "Oh, Grandmother, you must be very ill, for what a black nose you have."

"Better to smell your basket of goodies, my dear," said the wolf in his best grandmother voice.

"What a harsh voice you have, Grandmother," said the little girl, moving closer to the bed.

"You know I have been sick," said the wolf. It was at this point that he made his mistake. Just as Little Red reached the side of the bed. . .she was almost close enough now. . .the wolf couldn't resist playing the part of a sick old lady, and he wiped his brow with a hairy paw.

"My grandmother does not have hairy hands and dark hair on her arms," said Little Red. Her voice rose, "You are not my grandmother! What are you doing in her bed? and where is she?" cried the very scared girl as she ran to the door. "Help, help," she yelled as she fled.

A friendly woodcutter heard her cries and came hurrying with his axe. He saw a small girl running from the house and rushed in just in time to see a wolf rising from the bed, wearing a nightdress and a nightcap! "Here now, what's this?" he cried, raising his axe above his head.

The wolf was so frightened that he gave a big hiccup, and out jumped grandmother! The wolf then ran out of the house with the woodcutter right behind him. The last that Little Red and her grandmother saw of them was when they disappeared over a distant hill. The axe was still raised and so was the nightdress so the wolf would not trip.

I've embellished this story some to give you an opportunity to make your reading more dramatic. Children love drama. They like to pretend that what they are hearing is real.

Of course, children of a young age will not be able to use the methods of interpretation presented earlier, but they'll enjoy talking about stories and using their imaginations as they discuss parts of them.

There are no absolute rules in this very exciting time you are going to have except one, that your reader must have fun. Your young reader will learn to enjoy talking about what you read aloud and what is read silently if you are seen having fun with the stories.

There are any number of fun ways this story can be discussed. Some of the possibilities are demonstrated in the following conversations.

Teacher: *It's a funny picture I get in my mind when I see that wolf holding up the nightdress and running full tilt over the hill.*
Reader: *How would a wolf know to do that, anyway?*
Teacher: *He could have read about it in a story about a little girl who dresses up like a wolf and hides in an old grandmother wolf's bed to—*
Reader: *Oh, stop that. That's the same story, only about wolves.*
Teacher: *Right, sorry. Now this was a very smart wolf. What would you do if you were walking in the woods and you saw a wolf leaning against a tree?*
Reader: *I'd run.*

Teacher: But then there wouldn't be any story.
Reader: What story?
Teacher: The one where your grandmother is sick.
Reader: I'm not in a story. You said. . .
Teacher: What about that wolf eating grandmother and then she jumps out again and is okay?
Reader: I don't believe that part.
Teacher: Do you believe any of the story?
Reader: No. It's just a story. You're not supposed to believe it.
Teacher: Didn't you believe what I read? Do you think I changed some of it?
Reader: No. You probably read what was there.
Teacher: Was the wolf a bad wolf?
Reader: He was sneaky.
Teacher: Is that bad?
Reader: Not for a wolf.
Teacher: I like to think of that wolf in bed with a nightdress and a nightcap on and jumping up when the wood chopper comes in. That must have been funny looking.
Reader: We could put pj's on the dog and put him in the bed and see what he looks like.
Teacher: That's a good idea, but what do we do for a grandmother?
Reader: What do we need one for?
Teacher: For the dog to eat.
Reader: We wouldn't do that!

Below is a discussion of this same story with a very young Reader:

Teacher: Some bad things happen in that story, don't they?
Reader: They sure do.
Teacher: Can you list the things that happen that are bad?
Reader: The wolf eats the grandmother.
Teacher: Do you remember what I asked you to do?
Reader: Tell what happened that was bad.
Teacher: Not quite what I said. Let me ask again and you see if you can see a difference between what you just did and what I say. Can you list the things that are bad?
Reader: Sure, I did. I said the wolf ate the grandmother.
Teacher: Is that a list?
Reader: Oh, I see. Okay, here goes. Little Red Riding Hood meets a wolf in the woods. That's bad. Then Little Red Riding Hood lies to the wolf. That's not so good. Then the wolf eats the grandmother. There, that's a list.
Teacher: Good for you. You made quite a list. Let me ask you questions about other things and you figure out in the list where they should go.
Reader: How will I know where to put them?
Teacher: In the order in which they happen in the story.
Reader: What does that mean?

Teacher: The first thing bad that happens first, then the second thing that happens second, and so on.

Reader: I see. Okay, go ahead.

Teacher: The wood chopper raises his axe to strike a living thing?

Reader: That's a bad thing to do? He was saving Little Red Riding Hood.

Teacher: Okay. That's not a bad thing. How about this, the wolf gets in the grandmother's bed?

Reader: That's after he puts on the bedclothes.

Teacher: The wolf eats the grandmother?

Reader: That's before he puts on the bedclothes and . . .after he lies to the grandmother.

Teacher: Little Red Riding Hood talks to a stranger in the forest?

Reader: That's the wolf. That's near the start of her walk through the woods.

Teacher: The wood chopper tries to kill the wolf?

Reader: After the wolf tries to eat Little Red Riding Hood.

Teacher: You've a long list of things that happen in this story. Good for you.

Teacher then has the following conversation with a much younger child.

Reader: That's not a good story at all.

Teacher: Why not?

Reader: The writer's against women.

Teacher: How do you know that?

Reader: It's just like you taught me. Any story that makes fun of women or doesn't treat women fairly is not a good story.

Teacher: How does this story treat women?

Reader: Like they're all stupid.

Teacher: Give me an example.

Reader: The mother lets Little Riding Hood walk through the forest alone when she knows there are dangerous things out there.

Teacher: Okay, good. I missed that. What else?

Reader: Little Red talks to a wolf. She knows she isn't supposed to do that. Besides, wolves don't talk.

Teacher: I agree with the first part, that she shouldn't talk to the wolf, but the second part, about wolves not talking; I can't agree with that because in this story wolves do talk.

Reader: Little Red doesn't recognize that it's not her grandmother in the bed right away. The part about the black nose makes her seem stupid.

Teacher: I agree. She should have guessed that there was something wrong then.

Reader: The grandmother should recognize that it isn't Little Red's voice. Little Red would just walk in, she wouldn't knock. And she wouldn't say, "It is I, Little Red Riding Hood."

Teacher: Okay, what would she say?

Reader: "It's me, Grandmother."

Teacher: That makes sense.

Reader: I just don't like that story.

Teacher: *That's okay. You don't have to like every story, and you have good reasons for not liking it. I don't think too much of it now, either. Here's something to think about.*
Reader: *What?*
Teacher: *What if the wolf is a female wolf. What of the story then? Would you like it better?*
Reader: *I don't think it would make any difference what kind of a wolf it is. The story would still insult women.*
Teacher: *Don't you believe in the bogeywoman?*
Reader: *There's no such thing as a bogeywoman.*
Teacher: *Just bogeyman? That's as bad for men as the story is for women.*
Reader: *That's not fair!*

One of the problems you may have is to know when your reader is ready for more challenging discussions. The following is a conversation with a reader who feels too sophisticated for this story and is ready for something more complicated.

Reader: *Does the wolf get away?*
Teacher: *Do you want him to ?*
Reader: *Sure, he's a rare wolf. One of the last of the talking kind.*
Teacher: *An endangered species?*
Reader: *And he probably has a grandmother wolf and a little girl he calls Little Red Riding Wolf.*
Teacher: *Do you think there are people who come to his house to eat him?*
Reader: *No. They eat pizza and German chocolate cake. . .and drink red pop!*
Teacher: *What kind of a guy do you think the woodcutter is?*
Reader: *What's he doing with an axe. Where's his chain saw?*
Teacher: *Does he do the right thing when he chases the wolf away?*
Reader: *Sure he does. Otherwise the wolf would eat Little Red Riding Hood.*
Teacher: *What do you think about the scene in the woods when Little lies to the wolf? Is that okay to do?*
Reader: *Little?*
Teacher: *The little girl.*
Reader: *You call her Little?*
Teacher: *That's her name, isn't it? Little Red Riding Hood?*
Reader: *Oh, you think her first name is Little?*
Teacher: *It says that right in the story.*
Reader: *Then her last name is Hood?*
Teacher: *Sure, the Hood family. There's Father Hood, Mother Hood and Little Hood.*
Reader: *Her middle names are Red and Riding?*
Teacher: *Yep.*
Reader: *You think she might even have a brother named Robin?*
Teacher: *Sure.*
Reader: *That's crazy!*

Obviously this reader is not challenged enough by the story and is thinking creatively about things other than interpretation.

THE NOTORIOUS JUMPING FROG
OF
CALAVERAS COUNTY

In compliance with the request of a friend of mine, who wrote me from the East, I called on good-natured, garrulous old Simon Wheeler, and inquired after my friend's friend, Leonidas W. Smiley, as requested to do, and I herenunto append the result. I have a lurking suspicion that Leonidas W. Smiley is a myth, that my friend never knew such a personage, and that he only conjectured that if I asked old Wheeler about him, it would remind him of his infamous Jim Smiley, and he would go to work and bore me to death with some exasperating reminiscence of him as long and as tedious as it should be useless to me. If that was the design, it succeeded.

I found Simon Wheeler dozing comfortable by the bar-room stove of the dilapidated tavern in the decayed mining camp of Angel's, and I noticed that he was fat and bald-headed, and had an expression of winning gentleness and simplicity upon his tranquil countenance. He groused up, and gave me good day. I told him that a friend of mine had commissioned me to make some inquires about a cherished companion of his boyhood named Leonidas—Rev. Leonidas W. Smiley, a young minister of the Gospel, who he had heard was at one time a resident of Angel's Camp. I added that if Mr. Wheeler could tell me anything about this Rev. Leonidas W. Smiley, I would feel under many obligations to him.

Simon Wheeler backed me into a corner and blockaded me there with his chair, and then sat down and reeled off the monotonous narrative which follows this paragraph. He never smiled, he never frowned, he never changed his voice from the gentle-flowing key to which he tuned his initial sentence, he never betrayed the slightest suspicion of enthusiasm; but all through the interminable narrative there ran a vain of impressive earnestness and sincerity, which showed me plainly that, so far from his imagining that there was anything ridiculous or funny about his story, he regarded it as a really important matter, and admired its two heroes as men of transcendent genius in finesse. I let him go on in his own way, and never interrupted him once.

"Rev. Leonidas W., Reverend Le—well, there was a feller here once by the name of Jim Smiley, in the winter of '49—or maybe it was the spring of '50—I don't recollect exactly, somehow, though what makes me think it was one or the other is because I remember the big flume warn't finished when he first come to the camp; but anyway, he was the curiousest man about always betting on anything that turned up you ever see, if he could get anybody to bet on the other side; and if he couldn't he'd change sides. Any way that suited the other man would suit him—any way just so's he got a bet, he was satisfied. But still he was lucky, uncommon lucky; he most always come out winner. He was always ready and laying for a chance; there couldn't be no solit'ry thing mentioned but that fella'd offer to bet on it, and take ary side you please, as I was just telling you. If there was a horse-race, you'd find him flush or you'd find him busted at the end of it; if there was a dog-fight, he'd bet on it; if there was a cat-fight, he'd bet on it; if there was a chicken-fight, he'd bet on it; why, if there was two birds setting on a fence, he would bet you which one would fly first; or if there was a camp-meeting, he would be there reg'lar to bet on Parson Walker, which he judged to be the best exhorter about here, and so he was too, and a good man. If he even see a straddle-bug start to go anywheres, he would bet you how long it would take him to get to-to wherever he was going to, and if you took him up, he would foller that straddlebug to Mexico but what he would find out where he was bound for and how long he was on the road. Lots of the boys here has seen that Smiley, and can tell you about him. Why, it never made no difference to him—he'd bet on any thing—the dangdest feller.

Parson Walker's wife laid very sick once, for a good while, and it seemed as if they warn't going to save her; but one morning he come in, and Smiley up and asked him how she was, and he said she was considerable better-thank the Lord for his inf'nite mercy—and coming on so smart that with the blessing of Prov'dence she'd get well yet; and Smiley, before he thought, says, 'Well, I'll resk two-and-a-half she don't anyway.'

"Thish-yer Smiley had a mare—the boys called her the fifteen-minute nag, but that was only in fun, you know, because of course she was faster than that—and he used to win money on that horse, for all she was so slow and always had the asthma, or the distemper, or the consumption, or something of that kind. They used to give her two or three hundred yards start, and then pass her under way; but always at the fag end of the race she'd get excited and desperate like, and come cavorting and straddling up, and scattering her legs around limber, sometimes in the air, and sometimes out to one side among the fences, and kicking up m-o-r-e dust and raising m-o-r-e racket with her coughing and sneezing and blowing her nose—and always fetch up at the stand just about a neck ahead, as near as you could cipher it down.

"And he had a little small bull-pup that to look at him you'd think he warn't worth a cent but to set around and look ornery and lay for a different dog; his under-jaw'd begin to stick out like the fo'castle of a steamboat, and his teeth would uncover and shine like the furnaces. And a dog might tackle him and bully-rag him, and bite him and throw him over his shoulder two or three times, and Andrew Jackson—which was the name of the pup—Andrew Jackson would never let on but what he was satisfied, and hadn't expected nothing else—and the bets being doubled and doubled on the other side all the time, till the money were all up; and then all of a sudden he would grab that other dog jest by the j'int of his hind leg and freeze to it—not chaw, you understand, but only just grip and hang on till they throwed up the sponge, if it was a year. Smiley always come out winner on that pup, till he harnessed a dog once that didn't have no hind legs, because they'd been sawed off in a circular saw, and when the thing had gone along far enough, and the money was all up, and he come to make a snatch for his pet holt, he see in a minute how he'd been imposed on, and how that there dog had him in the door, so to speak, and he 'peared surprised, and then he looked sorter discouraged-like, and didn't try no more to win the fight, and so he got shucked out bad. He give Smiley a look, as much as to say his heart was broke, and it was his fault, for putting up a dog that hadn't no hind legs for him to take holt of, which was his main dependence in a fight, and then he limped off a piece and laid down and died. It was a good pup, was that Andrew Jackson, and would have made a name for hisself if he'd lived, for the stuff was in him and he had genius—I know it, because he hadn't no opportunities to speak of, and it don't stand to reason that a dog could make such a fight as he could under them circumstances if he hadn't no talent. It always makes me feel sorry when I think of that last fight of his'n, and the way it turned out.

"Well, this-yer Smiley had rat-terriers, and chicken cocks, and tomcats and all them kind of things, till you couldn't rest, and you couldn't fetch nothing for him to bet on but he'd match you. He ketched a frog one day, and took him home, and said he cal'lated to educate him; and so he never done nothing for three months but set in his back yard and learn that frog to jump. And you bet you he did learn him, too. He'd give him a little punch behind, and the next minute you'd see that frog whirling in the air like a doughnut—see him turn one summerset, or maybe a couple, if he got a good start, and come down flat-footed and all right, like a cat. He got him up so in the matter of ketching flies, and kep' him in practice so constant, that he'd nail a fly every time as fur as he could see him. Smiley said all a frog wanted was education, and he could do 'most anything—and I believe him. Why, I've seen him set Dan'l Webster down here on this floor—Dan Webster was the name of the frog—and sing out, 'Flies, Dan'l, flies!' and quicker'n you could wink he'd spring straight up and snake a fly off'n the counter there, and flop down on the floor ag'in as solid as a gob of mud, and fall to scratching the side of his head with his hind foot as indifferent as if he hadn't no idea he'd been doin' any more'n any frog might do. You never see a frog so modest and straightfor'ard as he was, for all he was so gifted. And when it come to fair and square jumping on a dead level, he could get over more ground at one straddle than any animal of his breed you ever see. Jumping on a dead level was his strong suit, you understand; and when it come to that, Smiley would ante up money on him as long as he had a red. Smiley was monstrous proud of his frog, and well he might be, for fellers that had traveled and been everywheres all said he laid over any frog that ever they see.

"Well, Smiley kep' the beast in a little lattice box, and he used to fetch him down-town sometimes and lay for a bet. One day a feller—a stranger in the camp, he was—come acrost him with his box, and says:

"`What might it be that you've got in the box?'

"And Smiley says, sorter indifferent-like, `It might be a parrot, or it might be a canary, maybe, but it ain't—it's only just a frog.'

"And the feller took it, and looked at it careful, and turned it round this way and that, and says, `H'm—so 'tis. Well, what's he good for?'

"`Well,' Smiley says, easy and careless, `he's good enough for one thing, I should judge—he can out jump any frog in Calaveras County.'

"The feller took the box again, and took another long, particular look, and give it back to Smiley, and says, very deliberate, `Well,' he says, `I don't see no p'ints about that frog that's any better'n any other frog.'

"`Maybe you don't,' Smiley says. `Maybe you understand frogs and maybe you don't understand 'em; maybe you've had experience, and maybe you ain't only a amature, as it were. Anyways, I've got my opinion, and I'll resk forty dollars that he can out jump any frog in Calaveras County.'

"And the feller studied a minute, and then says, kinder sad-like, `Well, I'm only a stranger here, and I ain't got no frog; but if I had a frog, I'd bet you.'

"And then Smiley says, 'That's all right—that's all right—if you'll hold my box a minute, I'll go and get you a frog.' And so the feller took the box, and put up his forty dollars along with Smiley's, and set down to wait.

"So he set there a good while thinking and thinking to himself, and then he got the frog out and prized his mouth open and took a teaspoon and filled him full of quail-shot—filled him pretty near up to his chin—and set him on the floor. Smiley he went to the swamp and slopped around in the mud for a long time, and finally he ketched a frog, and fetched him in, and give him to this feller, and says:

"`Now, if you're ready, set him alongside of Dan'l, with his fore paws just even with Dan'l's, and I'll give the word.' Then he says, `One—two—three—git!' and him and the feller touched up the frogs from behind, and the new frog hopped off lively, but Dan'l gave a heave, and hysted up his shoulders—so—like a Frenchman, but it warn't no use—he couldn't budge; he was planted as solid as a church, and he couldn't no more stir than if he was anchored out. Smiley was a good deal surprised, and he was disgusted too, but he didn't have no idea what the matter was, of course.

"The feller took the money and started away; and when he was going out at the door, he sorta jerked his thumb over his shoulder—so—at Dan'l, and says again very deliberate, `Well,' he says, `I don't see no p'ints about that frog that's any better'n any other frog.'

"Smiley he stood scratching his head and looking down at Dan'l a long time, and at last he says, "I do wonder what in the nation that frog throw'd off for—I wonder if there ain't something the matter with him—he 'pears to look mighty baggy, somehow.' And he ketched Dan'l by the nap of the neck, and hefted him, and says, 'Why blame my cats if he don't weight five pound!' and turned him upside down and he belched out a double handful of shot. And then he see how it was, and he was the maddest man—he set the frog down and took out after that feller, but he never ketched him. And—"

Here simon Wheeler heard his name called from the front yard, and got up to see what was wanted. And turning to me as he moved away, he said: "Just set where you are, stranger, and rest easy—I ain't going to be gone a second."

But, by your leave, I did not think that a continuation of the history of the enterprising vagabond Jim Smiley would be likely to afford me much information concernin the Rev. Leonidas W. Smiley, and so I started away.

At the door I met the sociable Wheeler returning, and he buttonholed me and recommended:

"Well, this-yer Smiley had a yaller one-eyed cow that didn't have no tail, only just a short stump like a bannanner, and —"

However, lacking both time and inclination, I did not wait to hear about the afflicted cow, but took my leave.

There are opportunities here to explore lots of different ways of understanding a story. The author, Twain:
1. Creates a very unusual character
2. Makes much use of regional dialect, even to the extent of making fun of dialects in fiction
3. Writes a story within a story
4. Presents an ironic situation
5. Creates humor through frustration of the reader and the narrator (narrative voice)
6. Doesn't have a clearly defined conflict
7. Leaves one of the characters "up in the air"
8. Foreshadows the events

The following conversations between Teacher and Reader explore some of these conditions in this attempt by Teacher to help Reader understand and enjoy humorous fiction.

Teacher: The voice telling this story was also a character in the story. Do you find that confusing?
Reader: No. That seems natural to me. In fact, I liked it.
Teacher: Why?
Reader: I don't know. It makes it more believable to have the person right there who it happened to.
Teacher: I hear you using the past tense there. Aren't we supposed to talk about the events in a story in present tense?
Reader: Sure, but I did. The narrative voice talks and we talk about him saying things in the present tense. But, he talks about things that happened to him in the past. We have to talk about those things that happened to him in the past, in past tense, don't we?
Teacher: Is that what you did?
Reader: Yes. I said, "It makes it more believable to have the person right there who it happened to." When I started that sentence I used present tense "it makes" and then switched to past tense with "it happened to," so I used present tense to talk about events in the story but past tense to talk about things the narrative voice told about that happened in the past. Isn't that the right way to do it?
Teacher: Sounds good to me.

Notice that Teacher has a discussion direction in mind at the beginning of this conversation. The intent is to talk about a narrative voice using first person and being involved in the action of the story. The conversation gets side-tracked, as many do, and they end up talking about tenses. This is fine. Reader is talking about the story in an intelligent way and is understanding it on a pretty sophisticated level.

Humor is a hard thing to talk about. What's funny to one person very often is not funny to another. In the following conversation Teacher tries to talk about what is funny in Twain's story and has some trouble being understood. A not unusual situation.

Teacher: That's a funny story. Not what I call a "knee slapper" but good just the same.
Reader: What's funny about it?
Teacher: The characters. Don't you think they're funny?
Reader: Interesting, yes. Funny, no.
Teacher: Oh boy. Something's wrong here. You don't find Jim Smiley, the old man in the store who talks all about this betting man, funny?
Reader: No. He talked all the time and didn't say much. He had a funny way of leaving out letters and sounds in his words. He wouldn't let anyone else talk. He captured a listener. But, he wasn't funny.
Teacher: Irony is the basis of much humor. Do you find the irony in the story funny?
Reader: What irony?
Teacher: Do you remember what irony is?

Reader: Sure, but talk about it for a minute just the same.

Teacher: Irony is when the opposite to what is expected happens. When one person tries to do something to another person and it happens to the first person instead. It's when I try to throw a pie in your face and it slips and lands on my head. That's ironic.

Reader: Some of this happens in the story?

Teacher: Sure it does. What kind of a man is Simon Wheeler talking about when he talks about Jim Smiley?

Reader: The betting man?

Teacher: Yes. What kind of a man is he?

Reader: He bets all the time and usually wins.

Teacher: What happens in the story that Simon tells about the stranger?

Reader: The stranger puts lead in Simon's frog and the frog can't jump.

Teacher: No irony there yet?

Reader: Nope.

Teacher: Simon usually wins one way or another doesn't he?

Reader: Yes.

Teacher: Remember the horse? It was really a fast horse but didn't look like it. Simon won lots of money betting on that horse. I'm not sure that was all that fair.

Reader: I see now. Simon won most of his bets even if he had to cheat a little, and when the stranger came to town, he beat Simon at his own game. . .Irony!

Teacher: Good for you. People enjoy irony because there's an element of justice in it. In this case, Simon gets what he deserves. He gets done to him what he's in the habit of doing to other people.

Reader: What's funny about that?

Teacher: That's a complicated question. Do you really want to know?

Reader: Sure.

Teacher: No one knows for sure why we laugh at things, but there are three main theories about laughter. They are: 1) we laugh at processes that are interrupted; 2) we laugh at unexpected turns of events; and 3) we laugh at those situations about which we have tensions. The most popular one, the one accepted by most people who study humor, is number three. This means that if we don't have tension about a subject, we won't laugh at a situation in that subject.

Reader: Is that why some of the jokes I tell you because I think they're funny, you don't like?

Teacher: That's a complicated way of putting it, but that's right. Different tensions produce different responses to situations.

Reader: How does that apply to this story?

Teacher: There are a number of things in the story that some people would think are funny. We were talking earlier about the irony in the story and how I thought the story was funny because of it.

Reader: About Jim Smiley getting done to him what he was used to doing to other people?

Teacher: Right. If a person doesn't have tension about justice in the world, and many children don't, ironic situations wouldn't seem funny to them. The people who would find the most humor in ironic situations are people who feel there's little justice in this life or people who, from their experiences, feel there's no justice.

103

Reader: And then they would laugh at the irony of the story?
Teacher: Yes.
Reader: I think I understand, but I don't think it's funny.

Characters are fun to discuss with young readers. They like to talk about why people do the things they do. Maybe we're all interested in motivations. Reader in the following conversation learns something about real people by talking about the characters in this story.

Reader: Strange characters in this story. I feel I know people just like them.
Teacher: Just like which ones?
Reader: The narrator of the second story about Jim Smiley, Simon Wheeler. He talks, and talks, and talks.
Teacher: What has Twain done that goes along with a person talking all the time.
Reader: What do you mean?
Teacher: What does Twain have Wheeler do with his body that a person who talks all the time would do?
Reader: He blockades the narrative voice of the main story with his chair. He captures him so he'll have an audience. That's just like Uncle Harry does. He gets you off in a corner and puts his back to the rest of the room and talks to you until even I can see that you want to get away.
Teacher: Is it that obvious?
Reader: Sure it is. Just as it's obvious to the narrator what Simon is doing. He even says that Wheeler backs him into a corner and blockades him there with his chair. Could we send this story to Uncle Harry?
Teacher: Would that be kind to your mother's brother?
Reader: Let's not. But there are people like that; we know some.
Teacher: That's why we enjoy reading about them. If we didn't recognize people like the ones in fiction, the stories wouldn't be so entertaining. What else does Twain have Wheeler do that is characteristic of that kind of a person—a compulsive talker?
Reader: He never lets up. He doesn't ask questions or give his listener a chance to say anything at all.
Teacher: What else?
Reader: When he's called away he says to his listener that he'll be right back and not to move. He wants an audience for when he gets back. Probably all the people in town know him and avoid him just like we all avoid Uncle Harry.
Teacher: I didn't know you did that, too.

Anton Chekhov is considered one of the greatest writers of all time and is enjoyed by most adults and older children who like to read. His understanding of character motivations is what makes his stories loved by so many people.

THE BET

It was a dark autumn night. The old banker was pacing from corner to corner of his study, recalling to his mind the party he had given in the fall fifteen years before. There were many clever people at the party and much interesting conversation. They talked among other things of capital punishment.

The guests, among them some scholars and journalists, for the most part disapproved of capital punishment. They found it obsolete as a means of punishment, unfitted to a Christian state and immoral. Some of them thought that capital punishment should be replaced universally by life imprisonment.

"I don't agree with you," said the host. "I myself have experienced neither capital punishment nor life imprisonment, but if one may judge a priori, then in my opinion capital punishment is more moral and more humane than imprisonment. Execution kills instantly; life imprisonment kills by degree. Who is the more humane executioner, one who kills you in a few seconds or one who draws the life out of you incessantly, for years?"

"They're both equally immoral," remarked one of the guests, "because their purpose is the same, to take away life. The state is not God. It has no right to take away that which it cannot give back, if it should so desire."

Among the company was a lawyer, a young man of about twenty-five. On being asked his opinion, he said: "Capital punishment and life imprisonment are equally immoral; but if I were offered the choice between them, I would certainly choose the second. It's better to live somehow than not to live at all."

There ensued a lively discussion. The banker, who was then younger and more nervous, suddenly lost his temper, banged his fist on the table, and turning to the young lawyer, cried out, "It's a lie. I bet you two millions you wouldn't stick in a cell even for five years."

"If you mean it seriously," replied the lawyer, "then I bet I'll stay not five but fifteen."

"Fifteen! done!" cried the banker. "Gentleman, I ask you all to be witnesses. I stake two millions."

"Agreed. You stake two millions, I my freedom," said the lawyer.

So this wild, ridiculous bet came to pass. The banker, a spoiled and capricious man, who at that time had too many millions to count, was beside himself with rapture. During Supper he said to the lawyer jokingly: "Come to your senses, young man, before it's too late. Two millions are nothing to me, but you stand to lose three or four of the best years of your life. I say three or four, because you'll never stick it out nay longer. Don't forget either, you unhappy man, that voluntary is much heavier than enforced imprisonment. The idea that you have the right to free yourself at any moment will poison the whole of your life in the cell. I pity you."

And now, fifteen years later, the banker, pacing from corner to corner, recalled all this and asked himself: "Why did I make this bet? What's the good? The lawyer loses fifteen years of his life and I throw away two millions. Will it convince people that capital punishment is worse or better than imprisonment for life? No, no! all stuff and rubbish. On my part, it was the caprice of a well-fed man; on the lawyer's, pure greed of gold."

He recollected further what happened after the evening party. It was decided that the lawyer must undergo his imprisonment under the strictest observation, in a garden wing of the banker's house.

It was agreed that during the period he would be deprived of the right to cross the threshold, to see living people, to hear human voices, and to receive letters and newspapers. He was permitted to have a musical instrument, to read books, to write letters, to drink wine and smoke tobacco.

By agreement he could communicate, but only in silence, with the outside world through a little window specially constructed for this purpose. Everything he wanted—books, music, wine, he could receive in any quantity by sending a note through the window.

The agreement provided for all the minutest details; it made the confinement strictly solitary, and it obliged the lawyer to remain exactly fifteen years, from twelve o'clock of November 14th, 1870, to twelve o'clock on November 14th, 1885. The least attempt on his part to violate the conditions, to escape if only for two minutes before the time, freed the banker from the obligation to pay him the two millions.

During the first year of imprisonment, the lawyer, as far as it was possible to judge from his short notes, suffered terribly from loneliness and boredom. From his wing, day and night, came the sound of the piano. He rejected wine and tobacco.

"Wine," he wrote, "excites desires, and desires are the chief foes of a prisoner; besides, nothing is more boring than to drink good wine alone," and tobacco spoiled the air in his room. During the first year the lawyer was sent books of a light character; novels with a complicated love interest, stories of crime and fantasy, comedies, and so on.

In the second year the piano was heard no longer and the lawyer asked only for classics. In the fifth year, music was heard again, and the prisoner asked for wine.

Those who watched him said that during the whole of that fifth year he was engaged only in eating, drinking, and lying on his bed. He yawned so often and talked angrily to himself. Books he did not read. Sometimes, at night, he would sit down to write. He would write for a long time, but then he would tear it all up in the morning. More than once he was heard to weep.

In the second half of the sixth year, the prisoner began zealously to study languages, philosophy, and history. He fell on these subjects so hungrily that the banker hardly had time to get books enough for him. In the space of four years about six hundred volumes were brought at his request.

It was while that passion lasted that the banker received the following letter from the prisoner: "My dear jailer, I am writing these lines in six languages. Show them to experts. Let them read them. If they do not find one single mistake, I beg you to give orders to have a gun fired off in the garden. By the noise I shall know that my efforts have not been in vain. The geniuses of all ages and countries speak in different languages, but in them all burns the same flame. Oh, if you knew my heavenly happiness now that I can understand them!"

The prisoner's desire was fulfilled. Two shots were fired in the garden by the banker's orders.

Later on, after the tenth year, the lawyer sat immovable before his table and read only the *New Testament*. The banker found it strange that a man, who in four years had mastered six hundred erudite volumes, should spend nearly a year in reading one book, easy to understand

and by no means thick. The *New Testament* was followed by the history of religions and theology.

During the last two years of his confinement, the prisoner read an extraordinary amount, quite haphazardly. Now he would apply himself to the natural sciences; then he would read Byron or Shakespeare. Notes used to come from him in which he asked to be sent at the same time a book on chemistry, a textbook of medicine, a novel, and some treatise on philosophy or theology.

He read as though he were swimming in the sea among broken pieces of wreckage, and in his desire to save his life was eagerly grasping one piece after another.

The banker recalled all this, and thought, "Tomorrow at twelve o'clock he receives his freedom. Under the agreement, I shall have to pay him two millions. If I pay, it's all over with me. I am ruined forever. . ."

Fifteen years before he had too many millions to count, but now he was afraid to ask himself which he had more of, money or debts. Gambling on the stock exchange, risky speculation, and the recklessness of which he could not rid himself even in his old age, had gradually brought his business to decay, and the fearless, self-confident, proud man of business had become an ordinary banker, trembling at every rise and fall in the market.

"That cursed bet," murmured the old man, clutching his head in despair. "Why didn't the man die? He's only forty years old. He will take away my last farthing, marry, enjoy life, gamble on the exchange, and I will look on like an envious beggar and hear the same words from him every day: `I'm obliged to you for the happiness of my life. Let me help you.' No, it's too much! The only escape from bankruptcy and disgrace—is that the man should die."

The clock had just struck three. The banker was listening. In the house every one was asleep, and one could hear only the frozen trees whining outside the windows. Trying to make no sound, he took out of his safe the key of the door which had not been opened for fifteen years, put on his overcoat, and went out of the house.

The garden was dark and cold. It was raining. A damp, penetrating wind howled in the garden and gave the trees no rest. Though he strained his eyes, the banker could see neither the ground, nor the white statues, nor the garden wing, nor the trees.

Approaching the garden wing, he called the watchman twice. There was no answer. Evidently the watchman had taken shelter from the bad weather and was now asleep somewhere in the kitchen or the greenhouse.

"If I have the courage to fulfill my intention," thought the old man, "the suspicion will fall on the watchmen first of all."

In the darkness he groped for the steps and for the door and entered the hall of the garden wing; then he poked his way into a narrow passage and struck a match. Not a soul was there, and an iron stove loomed dark in the corner. The seals on the door that led into the prisoner's room were unbroken.

When the match went out, the old man, trembling from agitation, peeped into the little window.

In the prisoner's room a candle was burning dimly. The prisoner himself sat by the table. Only his back, the hair on his head, and his hands were visible. Open books were strewn about on the table, on the two chairs, and on the carpet near the table.

Five minutes passed and the prisoner never once stirred. Fifteen years' confinement had taught him to sit motionless. The banker tapped on the window with his finger, but the prisoner made no movement in reply.

Then the banker cautiously tore the seals from the door and put the key into the lock. The rusty lock gave a hoarse groan and the door creaked. The banker expected instantly to hear a cry of surprise and the sound of steps. Three minutes passed and it was as quiet inside as it had been before. He made up his mind to enter.

Before the table sat a man, unlike an ordinary human being. It was a skeleton, with tightly drawn skin, with long curly hair like a woman's, and a shaggy beard. The color of his face was yellow, of an earthy shade; the cheeks were sunken, the back long and narrow, and the hand upon which he leaned his hairy head was so lean and skinny that it was painful to look upon. His hair was already silvering with gray, and no one who glanced at the senile emaciation of the face would have believed that he was only forty years old. On the table, before his bent head, lay a sheet of paper on which something was written in a tiny hand.

"Poor devil," thought the banker, "he's asleep and probably seeing millions in his dreams. I have only to take and throw this half-dead thing on the bed, smother him a moment with the pillow, and the most careful examination will find no trace of unnatural death. But, first let us read what he has written here."

The banker took the paper from the table and read:

Tomorrow at twelve o'clock midnight, I shall obtain my freedom and the right to mix with people. But before I leave this room and see the sun I think it is necessary to say a few words to you. On my own clear conscience and before God who sees me I declare to you that I despise freedom, life, hearth, and all that your books call the blessings of the world.

For fifteen years I have diligently studied earthly life. True, I saw neither the earth nor its people, but in your books I drank fragrant wine, sang songs, hunted deer and wild boar in the forests, loved women. . .And beautiful women, like clouds ethereal, created by the magic of your poets' genius, visited me by night and whispered to me wonderful tales, which made my head drunken. In your books I climbed the summits of Elbruz and Mont Blanc and saw from there how the sun rose in the morning, and in the evening suffused the sky, the ocean and the mountain ridges with a purple gold.

I saw from here how above me lightning glimmered cleaving the clouds; I saw green forests, fields, rivers, lakes, cities; I heard sirens singing, and the playing of the pipes of Pan; I touched the wings of beautiful visions who came flying to me to speak of God.

In your books I cast myself into bottomless abysses, worked miracles, burned cities to the ground, preached new religions, conquered whole countries. . .

Your books gave me wisdom. All that unwearying human thought has created through the centuries is compressed in a little lump in my skull. I know that I am wiser than off of you.

And I despise your books, despise all worldly blessings and wisdom. Everything is void, frail, visionary and delusive as a mirage. Though you be proud and wise and beautiful, yet will death wipe you from the face of the earth like the mice underground;

and your posterity, your history, and the immortality of your men of genius will be as frozen slag, burnt down together with the terrestrial globe.

You are mad, and gone the wrong way. You take falsehood for truth and ugliness for beauty. You would marvel if suddenly apple and orange trees should bear frogs and lizards instead of fruit, and if roses should begin to exude the odor of a sweating horse. So do I marvel at you, who have bartered heaven for earth. I do not want to understand you.

That I may show you in deed my contempt for that by which you live, I waive the two millions of which I once dreamed as of paradise, and which I now despise. That I may deprive myself of my right to them, I shall come out from here five minutes before the stipulated term and thus shall violate the agreement.

When he had finished, the banker put the document on the table, kissed the head of the strange man, and began to weep. He went out of the wing. Never at any other time, not even after his terrible losses on the exchange, had he felt such contempt for himself as now. Returning home, he lay down on his bed, but agitation and tears kept him a long time from sleeping. . .

The next morning the poor watchman came running to him and told him that he had seen the man who was locked in the wing climb through the window into the garden. He had gone to the gate and disappeared.

The banker instantly went with his servants to the wing and established the escape of the prisoner. To avoid unnecessary rumors he took the paper with the renunciation from the table, and, on his return, locked it in his safe.

Teacher: That's a sad and powerful story for me. How does it strike you?

Reader: I don't know what to think. Maybe I don't understand it. The lawyer stays in the room for fifteen years then just walks away. Why?

Teacher: He changes while he's locked up, doesn't he?

Reader: He sure does. When he first makes the bet, he's sure he'll stay for the fifteen years and walk away with two million dollars or rubles or something.

Teacher: The lawyer is what we call a dynamic character. One who changes in the course of the story. Not too common in short fiction, but it's very common for a character to change in a novel.

Reader: Why does he do that? Change, I mean?

Teacher: Something must happen to him while he's locked up. What does he do?

Reader: Not too much. He can't talk to people or even get letters. He can't see other people. He can play the piano and read.

Teacher: Could playing the piano change a person?

Reader: It might, but he doesn't play that much. What he does is read.

Teacher: What kind of reading?

Reader: All good things. He doesn't spend much time on popular books at all. He spends a whole year on the Bible.

Teacher: He must learn a lot about the values of life in all that reading. What does he say about the life that he runs away from?

Reader: That's hard to remember. Let me read it:

And I despise your books, despise all worldly blessings and wisdom.
Everything is void, frail, visionary and delusive as a mirage. Though
you be proud and wise and beautiful, yet will death wipe you from the
face of the earth like the mice underground and your posterity, your
history, and the immortality of your men of genius will be as frozen
slag, burnt down together with the terrestrial globe.

Teacher: *He hates everything, doesn't he?*

Reader: *I don't think everything. He says: "So do I marvel at you, who have bartered heaven*
for earth. I do not want to understand you." It seems that he still respects Heaven,
but that's all.

Teacher: *He has become what we call a nihilist?*

Reader: *What's that?*

Teacher: *Someone who denies any basis for truth or values.*

Reader: *I don't think so. He denies the values of the culture he runs away from.*

Teacher: *What's the banker's reaction to that?*

Reader: *The banker goes home and feels disgust for himself and cries for a long time.*

Teacher: *What other time had he felt such disgust with himself?*

Reader: *When he lost all his money on the stock exchange.*

Teacher: *How is this disgust like before?*

Reader: *He must feel he's lost something when the lawyer runs away from the money.*

Teacher: *What could that be?*

Reader: *He could have lost respect for what he believed in. For the values of his culture that*
the lawyer has learned to hate. He was so worried about losing his last two million
and the lawyer doesn't even want it. The banker is made to see that what he places
so much value in is not of much value at all.

Teacher: *That's good thinking.*

Reader: *I have a question about this. If the lawyer learns enough about life in his fifteen years*
of reading that he rejects what the banker loves and he doesn't want the money after
all, and the banker feels disgust for his values and what they have made him do, do
both men lose the bet?. . .or do they both win?

Teacher: *Wow! Such a good question. That's excellent thinking on your part. How do you feel*
about the bet?

Reader: *I think it was stupid. Two million of anything isn't worth fifteen years of anyone's*
life.

Teacher: *Can you think of any situation where a person might give fifteen years of life for two*
million?

Reader: *Sure, but not for himself. I can imagine a person doing that so someone else could*
live by having an operation. But that's not the case here. This was just for the money,
and neither man thinks it was really worth it. The banker doesn't think so at the start
of the bet, and the lawyer doesn't think so at the end of the bet.

Teacher: *Would you say that they both lose then?*

Reader: *It depends on what you value. If you think one way, then they both could have won.*

Teacher: *How could that be?*

TYPES OF STORIES

ADVENTURE   A story typified by great action, suspense and risk.

ALLEGORY   A story that uses fictional characters as symbols to teach abstract concepts, such as moral or spiritual lessons.

ANIMAL   *Realistic*, where the animals function as animals do in real life, or *Fantastic/Romantic*, where the animals function as if they were people or have characteristics not common to animals (speech, abstract thought, human emotions, etc.)

AUTOBIOGRAPHY   The story of a person's life written by that person.

BIOGRAPHY   The story of a person's life written by someone else.

FABLE   A brief narrative passed down through generations which usually contains a moral message.

FANTASY   A story which violates the known laws of science or nature.

HISTORICAL   Realistic recreation of some past time and/or place, often with fictional character in non-fiction setting.

HORROR   A concentration on frightful events or situations.

HUMAN INTEREST   A journalistic piece written with the intent of creating compassion, sympathy or empathy for a situation or people.

MYSTERY   A story that solves a puzzle or crime with a writing style that arouses curiosity or speculation.

MYTH   A story made up to explain what is not understood about some aspect of nature or human forces.

SCIENCE FICTION   A combination of science and imagination with a concentration on science.

Reader: If both men come to the realization that money and things are not of great value, not worth more than life, then that could be seen as a good thing by a person who thinks that way too. That person then could say that both men win the bet.

Teacher: Why?

Reader: Because both men come away from the bet with more than they start with. The banker wins because he has more things to value, and he still gets to keep his two million, and the lawyer wins because he gets more than the value of the two million. In fact so much more that he doesn't want or need the money.

Teacher: Okay, I see that. Now, how could they both lose?

Reader: That's easy. The lawyer loses the bet because he doesn't stay in the room as the bet says. The banker loses because, even though he is the technical winner, he loses more than the value of the money. We know this because, when he knows that he's the winner, he feels disgust with himself, just like the disgust he felt when he lost most of his money in stocks.

Teacher: Then, even though the men are in a betting contest, the real conflict isn't with them against each other?

Reader: It can't be. If it were, the banker wouldn't feel bad when he wins.

Teacher: So, the conflict here must be between the two men and some other force?

Reader: Yes. It's almost as if the two men are working together to battle the other side. They do this by betting on what is most valuable.

Teacher: What do they bet on?

Reader: On whether money or time is more valuable.

Teacher: I don't understand your identification of time as the value. Nobody bets time.

Reader: They both do. Fifteen years against two millions.

Teacher: Careful here. Nobody can take away fifteen years unless they were to kill the other person fifteen years before natural death would occur. And that's impossible to do.

Reader: I see what you mean. The lawyer still has the fifteen years. I know! He has the years but in confinement. He doesn't have fifteen years in the company of the banker and his friends in their society. That's the other side. What life is like outside of the prison.

Teacher: Good for you.

Reader: No, good for us. I don't think you knew that all along, did you?

ENGLISH WORD ROOTS

A familiarity with the common word roots will give your children an ability to analyze unfamiliar words and understand them by more than they might by just studying context. Obviously this in not a complete listing, only a sample of the most common roots.

ab	away from		geo	earth	
ad	to/toward		graph/gram	write	
agon	contest/struggle		hemi	half	
al	pertinent/suited to		homo	same	
an	without		hydra	water	
ante	before		inter	between	
anti	against		intra	within	
anthrop	human		iso	equal	
aqua	water		ity	condition/ quality	
ary	pertaining		ject	throw	
astr/aster	star		logos	word/study	
auto	self		mania	madness for	
bene	good/well		mater/matr	mother	
bi	two		med	middle	
biblio	book		meter	measure	
bio	life		micro	small	
capit	head		mill	thousand	
cardi1heart			mis	wrong	
cent	hundred		mit	send	
chloro	green		mono	one	
chron	time		non	not	
cid	kill		ob	against	
circum	around		ocul	eye	
com/con/col	together		omni	all	
contra/			onym	name	
contro	against		ophthalm	eye	
corpor	body		ora	mouth	
cracy/crat	rule/government		para	beside	
de	down/away from		pater/patr	father	
dis	separation/reversal		ped	foot	
dynam	power		pend	hang	
escent	becoming/growing		penta	five	
ex	out of/former		per	through	
flect/flex	bend		peri	around	
frater/fratr	brother		philo	love	
fy	make		phobia	fear of	
gen	kind		phon	sound	

phos/phot	light
pneum	air/wind/breath
poly	many
port	carry
post	after
pre	before
pro	before/forward
proto	first
quadr	four
re	back/again
retro	back
se	apart
scope	aim/view
sed	remain
semi	half
soph	wisdom
sub	under
super	above
syn	together
tele	far/distant
terr	earth
theo	God/god
thermos	heat
thesis	position/place
trans	across
tri	three
uni	one
ultra	beyond/excessive
un	not
video/vision	see

Common noun suffixes:
-ancy -dom -ency -hood
-ness -tion -ship

Common verb suffixes:
-ate -en -fy

Common adjective suffixes:
-ful -ish -ate -less
-ly

GLOSSARY OF LITERARY TERMS

CHARACTERS: The people or animals representing the forces in conflict.
Characterization - The creating of the characters in a story. Among others, the main methods are:
1. Describing or showing the character's physical traits and describing his or her personality.
2. Describing or showing the character's speech and behavior.
3. Describing other characters' reactions to the character.
4. Describing or giving the character's thoughts.

DIALECT: Speech typical of a specific locale.

DIALOGUE: Conversation between two or more characters or a conversation one character might have when alone. For instance, one between a woman and her conscience.

FLASHBACK: An interruption of the action to show an event which had occurred at an earlier time.

FORESHADOWING: The giving of clues (hints) of events that will happen in the future actions in the story.

IMAGERY: A description that gives the reader a picture of the action or location. Vivid imagery gives the reader the taste, sound, sight, feeling and smell of the event.

PARODY: The making fun of an author's writing by the copying and exaggerating of that author's writing characteristics.

PERSONIFICATION: The presentation of an animal or an object as if it had human characteristics: "The sad sighing of the sea."

POINT OF VIEW: The (perspective) which the narrative voice takes in relating the events of a story.

SATIRE: The making fun of the weaknesses in people, institutions, or situations by exaggeration of their characteristics.

SYMBOL: The using of a concrete object (like a flag) to represent an abstract concept (like a country).

A LISTING OF SUGGESTED BOOK AND STORY READINGS

This listing was suggested by a number of sources, the main one being a reading expert at Indiana University. Since university teachers don't view books the same way mothers do, I suggest you check the books on this list to make sure they are appropriate for your children. For instance, there are some ghost stories listed here, and all mothers don't want their children reading them.

PRE-READERS AND BEGINNING READERS

Isenberg	*Albert the Running Bear Gets the Jitters*	Zoloton	*The Poodle Who Barked at the Wind*
Carlson	*Arnie and the Stolen Markers*	Marshall	*Red Riding Hood*
Bassett	*Beany and Scamp*	Carrick	*Rosalie*
Rylant	*Birthday Presents*	Kraus	*Spider's First Day at School*
Littledale	*The Farmer in the Soup*	Anholt	*Truffles in Trouble*
Weinberg	*The Forgetful Bears Meet Mr. Memory*	Talbott	*We're Back! A Dinosaur's Story*
Adler	*The Fourth Floor Twins and the Skyscraper Parade*		
Keller	*Goodbye, Max*		
Wahl	*Humphrey's Bear*		
Blundell	*Joe on Sunday*		
Rutland	*Knights and Castles*		
Hafner	*M and M and the Super Child Afternoon*		
Winthrop	*Maggie and the Monster*		
Yamashita	*Mice at the Beach*		
Feller	*Midnight Snowman*		
Aiken	*The Moon's Revenge*		
Jance	*A More Perfect Union*		
Arnold	*No Jumping on the Bed*		
Pizer	*Nosey Gilbert*		
Brown	*Our Puppy's Vacation*		
Small	*Paper John*		
Titherington	*A Place for Ben*		

BEGINNING READERS

Brimner	*BMX Freestyle*
Mayer	*Baby Sister Says No*
Wiesman	*Barber Bear*
Boujon	*Bon Appetite, Mr Rabbit*
Birdwell	*Clifford's Christmas*
Carey	*The Devil and Mother Crump*
McPhair	*First Flight*
Cazet	*Frosted Glass*
Smith	*Grover and the New Kid*
Ziefert	*Harry Takes a Bath*
Munroe	*The Inside-Outside Book of Washington, D.C.*
Mayer	*Just a Mess*
Graham	*Mr. Bear's Chair*
Cole	*Norma Jean, Jumping Bean*
Christelow	*Olive and the Magic Hat*
Gretz	*Roger Takes Charge!*
San Souci	*Short & Shivery*
Ziefert	*So Hungry!*
Ross	*Stone Soup*
Stadler	*Three Cheers for Hippo!*
Ishii	*The Tongue-Cut Sparrow*
Tyler	*Waiting for Mom*
Ziefert	*Where is Nicky's Valentine?*
Handord	*Where's Waldo*

GRADE 1

Rabe	*The Balancing Girl*	Cole	*No More Baths*
Schwartz	*Begin at the Beginning*	Krause	*Noel the Coward*
Hoban	*Best Friends for Frances*	Hogrogian	*One Fine Day*
Mayer	*A Boy a Dog and a Frog*	Keats	*Over in the Meadow*
Sendak	*Chicken Soup With Rice*	Johnston	*The Quilt Story*
Aesop	*The City Mouse & the Country Mouse*	Scarry	*Richard's Scarry's Find Your ABC's*
Rey	*Curious George*	Hutchins	*Rosie's Walk*
Littledale	*The Elves and the Shoemaker*	Becker	*Seven Little Rabbits*
		Barrett	*A Snake is Totally Tail*
Goffstein	*Fish for Supper*	Babbitt	*The Something*
Brown	*Goodnight Moon*	Williams	*Something Special for Me*
Brown	*Gorilla*	Wells	*Stanley and Rhoda*
Tripp	*The Great Big Ugly Man Came Up & Tied His Horse to Me*	Galdone	*The Three Bears*
		McNaught	*Truck Book*
		Ryder	*Under the Moon*
Howard	*I Can Count to 100. Can You?*	Brenne	*Wagon Wheels*
		dePaola	*Watch Out for the Chicken Feet in Your Soup*
Virost	*I'll Fix Anthony*		
Oram	*In the Attic*	Udry	*What Mary Jo Shared*
Bradenburg	*I Wish I Was Sick Too!*	Reit	*When Small is Tall*
Cohen	*Jim's Dog Muffins*	Keats	*Whistle for Willie*
Burton	*Katy and the Big Snow*	Cohen	*Will I Have a Friend?*
Payne	*Katy No-Pocket*		
Patter	*Koko's Kitten*		
Piper	*The Little Engine That Could*		
Bornstein	*Little Gorilla*		
Dunn	*The Little Pig*		
Bemelmans	*Madeline*		
DeRegniers	*May I Bring a Friend?*		
Tresselt	*Mitten*		
Asch	*Mooncake*		
Bataglia	*Mother Goose*		
Phillips	*My New Boy*		
Moore	*Night Before Christmas*		
Cohen	*No Good in Art*		

GRADE 2

Simon	*Airplane Book*	Burton	*Mike Mulligan and His Steam Shovel*
Naylor	*All Because I'm Older*		
Parrish	*Amelia Bedelia*	Bonsall	*Mine's the Best*
Stevens	*Anna, Grandpa, and the Big Storm*	Lobel	*Ming Lo Moves the Mountain*
Gerstein	*Arnold of the Ducks*	Lobel	*Mouse Soup*
Brown	*Arthur's Teacher Trouble*	Drescher	*My Mother's Getting Married*
Haywood	*B is for Betsy*		
Dc Brunhoff	*Babar Saves the Day*	de Paola	*Nana Upstairs and Nana Downstairs*
Hoban	*A Bargain for Frances*		
Say	*The Bicycle Man*	Sharmat	*Nate the Great and the Fishy Prize*
Rockwell	*Big Boss*		
Cole	*Bony-Legs*	Wells	*Noisy Nora*
Spier	*Bored-Nothing to Do*	Raskin	*Nothing Ever Happens on My Block*
Giff	*The Case of the Cool-Itch Kid*		
		Kellogg	*Paul Bunyan*
Coatsworth	*The Cat Who Went to Heaven*	Weiss	*Princess Pearl*
		Marzollo	*Red Ribbon Rosie*
Slepian	*The Cat Who Wore a Pot on Her Head*	Willard	*Simple Pictures Are Best*
		Ryder	*The Snail's Spell*
Shub	*Clever Kate*	Levey	*Something Queer at the Ball Park*
Turner	*Dakota Dugout*		
Steig	*Dr. De Soto*	Potter	*Tale of Peter Rabbit*
Ehrich	*Emma's New Pony*	Blaine	*The Terrible Thing that Happened at Our House*
Ransome	*The Fool of the World and the Flying Ship*		
		Mayer	*There's a Nightmare in My Closet*
Heine	*Friends*		
Martin	*The Ghost-Eye Tree*	Phillips	*Tiger is a Scardy Cat*
Provensen	*The Glorious Flight*	Lingren	*Tomten*
Sharmat	*Gregory the Terrible Eater*	Crowe	*Tyler Toad and the Thunder*
		Carrick	*The Washout*
Brown	*Hansel and Gretel*	Rylant	*When I Was Young in the Mountains*
Zion	*Harry by the Sea*		
Aliki	*How a Book is Made*	Bonsall	*Who's a Pest?*
Waber	*Ira Sleeps Over*		
O'Connor	*Jackie Robinson*		
de Paola	*The Legend of the Bluebonnet*		
Kraus	*Leo the Late Bloomer*		
MacDonald	*The Little Island*		
Gramatky	*Little Toot*		

CALDECOTT MEDAL WINNERS

Awarded annually to the illustrator of the most distinguished picture book for children. Normally appropriate for 2nd - 5th graders

D'Aulaire	*Abraham Lincoln*	Yolen	*Owl Moon*
Leodhas	*Always Room for One More*	Hall	*Ox-Cart Man*
		Allsburg	*Polar Express*
Lathrop	*Animals of the Bible*	Field	*Prayer for a Child*
McDermott	*Arrow to the Sun: Indian Tale*	Petrsham	*Rooster Crow: A Book of American Rhymes and Jingles*
Musgrove	*Ashanti to Zulu*		
Robbins	*Baboushka and the Three Kings*	Hodges	*Saint George and the Dragon*
Hader	*Big Snow*	Ness	*Sam, Bangs & Moonshine*
Ward	*Biggest Bear*		
Macauly	*Black and White*	Cendrars	*Shadow*
Cooney	*Chanticleer and the Fox*	Diaz	*Smoky Night*
Emberley	*Drummer Hoff*	Keats	*Snowy Day*
Zemach	*Gee Tree*	Gammell	*Song and Dance Man*
Lobel	*Fables*	Steig	*Sylvester and the Magic Pebble*
Will	*Finders Keepers*		
Ransome	*Fool of the World and the Flying Ship*	Lawson	*They Were Strong and Good*
Langstaff	*Frog Went a Courtin'*	McCloskey	*Time of Wonder*
Goble	*Girl Who Loved Wild Horses*	Udry	*Tree is Nice*
		Wiesner	*Tuesday*
Provensen	*Glorious Flight*	Sendak	*Where the Wild Things Are*
Say	*Grandfather's Journey*		
Burton	*Little House*		
MacDonald	*Little Island*		
Young	*Lon Po Po*		
Blmelmans	*Make Way for Ducklings*		
Thruber	*Many Moons*		
McCully	*Mirette on the High Wire*		
Ets	*Nine Days to Christmas*		
Spier	*Noah's Ark*		
Rathmann	*Officer Buckle and Gloria*		
Brown	*Once a Mouse*		
Hogrogian	*One Fine Day*		

GRADE 3

Steven	*Anna, Grandpa and the Big Storm*	Levine	*If You Traveled on the Underground Railroad*
Anno	*Anno's Counting Book*	Baylor	*If You Are a Hunter of Fossils*
Titus	Basil and the Lost Colony	Keats	*John Henry: An American Legend*
Keith	*Bedita's Bad Day*	Cameron	*Julian, Secret Agent*
Robinson	*Best Christmas Pageant Ever*	Jukes	*Like Jake and Me*
Sharmat	*Big Fat Enormous Lie*	Davidson	*Louis Braille*
Allard	*Bumps in the Night*	Cole	*The Magic School Bus Inside the Earth*
Adler	*Cam Jasen and the Mystery at the Monkey House*	Wolkstein	*Magic Wings*
Cole	*Cars and How They Go*	Travers	*Mary Poppins*
Berends	*The Case for the Elevator Duck*	Isadora	*Max*
Smith	*Chocolate Fever*	Cleary	*Mouse and the Motorcycle*
Catling	*Chocolate Touch*	MacDonald	*Mrs. Piggle-Wiggle*
Hurvitz	*Class Clown*	Hogrogian	*One Fine Day*
Aliki	*Corn is Maize*	Holling	*Paddle-to-the-Sea*
Gorsline	*Cowboys*	Munsch	*The Paper Bag Princess*
Thaler	*Cream of Creature From the School Cafeteria*	Jeschke	*Perfect the Pig*
Sobol	*Encyclopedia Brown Finds the Clues*	Giff	*Rat Teeth*
		Griff	*Say "Cheese"*
		Christian	*Sebastian and the Secret of the Skewered Skier*
Wilder	*Farmer Boy*	Lauber	*Seeds: Pob Slick Glide*
Brown	*Flat Stanley*	Park	*Skinnybones*
Shreve	*Flunking of Joshua T. Bates*	Anderson	*The Smallest Life Around Us*
Adler	*Fourth Floor Twins and the Fish Snitch Mystery*	Carriak	*Stay Away From Simon*
		Cameron	*The Stories Julian Tells*
Dahl	*George's Marvelous Medicine*	Donnelly	*The Titanic: Lost. . .and Found*
Fatio	*The Happy Lion*	Shub	*White Stallion*
Kraske	*Harry Houdini*	Donnelly	*Who Shot the President?*
Selden	*Harry Kitten and Tucker Mouse*		
McGovern	*If You Grew Up With Abraham Lincoln*		

CORETTA SCOTT KING AWARD

Normally appropriate for 3rd - 7th graders

McKissack	*Christmas in the Big House, Christmas in the Quarters*
McKissack	*The Dark-thirty Southern Tales of the Supernatural*
Hamilton	*The Defeat and Triumph of a Fugitive Slave*
Clifton	*Everett Anderson's Goodbye*
Myers	*Fallen Angels*
Taylor	*The Friendship*
Draper	*Forged by Fire*
Johnson	*Heaven*
Hamilton	*Her Stories*
Walker	*Justin and the Best Biscuits in the World*
Taylor	*Let the Circle Be Unbroken*
McKissack	*A Long Hard Journey: The Story of the Pullman Porter*
McKissack	*Miranda and Brother Wind*
Myers	*Now is Your Time! The African-American Struggle*
Hamilton	*The People Could Fly: American Black Folktales*
Taylor	*The Road to Memphis*
Myers	*Slam!*
Hamilton	*Sweet Whispers, Brother Rush*
Stolz	*Thief in the Village and Other Stories*
Poitier	*This Life*
Johnson	*Toning the Sweep*
Greenfield	*Under the Sunday Tree*

GRADE 4

Park	*Almost Starting Skinnybones*	George	*My Side of the Mountain*
King-Smith	*Babe the Gallant Pig*	Saunders	*Mystery Cat*
Farley	*Black Stallion*	Sharmat	*Nate the Great and the Boring Beach Bag*
Henry	*Brighty of the Grand Canyon*	Horwitz	*Night Markets*
Stolz	*The Bully of Barkam Street*	Cooper	*Over Sea Under Stone*
		King-Smith	*Pigs Might Fly*
Allard	*Bumps in the Night*	Lindgren	*Pippi in the South Seas*
Franchere	*Cesar Chavez*	Lindgren	*Pippi Longstocking*
Bulla	*The Chalk Box Kid*	Kunhardt	*Pompeii—Buried Alive!*
Swan	*Destination: Antarctica*	Haas	*Poppy and the Outdoor Cat*
Dahl	*Dirty Beasts*		
Gilson	*Do Bananas Chew Gum?*	Cleary	*Ralph S. Mouse*
Wallace	*A Dog Called Kitty*	Conford	*Revenge of the Incredible Dr. Rancid & His Youthful Assistant, Jeffery*
Shura	*Don't Call Me Toad!*		
Green	*Eating Ice Cream With A Werewolf*		
Rodgers	*Freaky Friday*	Godden	*The Rocking Horse Mystery*
Davidson	*Frederick Douglass Fights for Freedom*	MacLachlan	*Sara Plain and Tall*
Fitzgerald	*Great Brain at the Academy*	Grillone	*Small Worlds Close Up*
		Bjorklund	*Snowshoe Trek to Otter River*
Walsh	*The Green Book*		
Lewis	*The Horse and His Boy*	Peck	*Soup*
Clymer	*Horse in the Attic*	Fitzhugh	*Sport*
Farber	*How Does it Feel to Be Old*	White	*Stuart Little*
		Blume	*Tales of a Fourth Grade Nothing*
Kurelek	*How to Eat Fried Worms*		
Burch	*Ida Early Comes Over the Mountain*	Garniner	*Top Secret*
		Sobol	*Two Minute Mysteries*
Bellairs	*Letter the Witch and the Ring*	Frost	*You Come Too*
Wilder	*Little House in the Big Woods*		
Laughlin	*Little Leftover Witch*		
Knowlton	*Maps & Globes*		
Aliki	*Medieval Feast*		
Donnelly	*Moonwalk*		
O'Brien	*Mrs. Frisby and the Rats of Nimh*		

MYSTERY WRITERS OF AMERICA

Edgar Allan Poe Award
Normally appropriate for 4th- 7th graders

Brookins	*Alone in Wolf Hollow*
Peck	*Are You in the House Alone?*
Voight	*Callender Papers*
Finlay	*Danger at Black Dyke*
Hamilton	*House of Dies Drear*
Shreve	*Lucy Forever and Miss Rosetree, Shrinks*
Nixon	*The Kidnapping of Christina Lattimore*
Roberts	*Megan's Island*
Branscum	*Murder of Hound Dog Bates*
Naylor	*Night Cry*
Nixon	*Other Side of the Dark*
Winsdor	*The Sandman's Eyes*
Nixon	*The Seance*
Mazer	*Taking Terri Mueller*
O'Brien	*Z for Zachariah*

GRADE 5

Konigsburg	Altogether One at a Time	Juster	*Phantom Tollbooth*
Lowery	*Anastasia Has the Answers*	King	*Pigs Might Fly*
		Pryor	*Rats Spiders and Love*
Hurwitz	*Baseball Fever*	Avi	*Romeo and Juliet Together (and alive!)*
Naylor	*Beetles Lightly Toasted*		
Cobb	*Bet You Can!*	DeJong	*Shadrach*
Farley	*Black Stallion Returns*	Byers	*Summer of the Swans*
Norton	*The Borrowers*	Mebs	*Sunday's Child*
Paterson	*Bridge to Tarabithia*	Johnston	*They Led the Way*
Benjamin	*Cartooning for Kids*	Smith	*War With Grandpa*
Stolz	*Cat in the Mirror*		
Girion	*Chicken Bone Wish*		
Boston	*The Children of Green Knoll*		
Fleming	*Chitty Chitty Bang Bang*		
Boyd	*Circle of Gold*		
Byars	*Cracker Jackson*		
Clearly	*Dear Mr. Henshaw*		
Wright	*The Dollhouse Murders*		
Wright	*Getting Rid of Marjorie*		
Green	*A Girl Called Al*		
Pogany	*The Golden Fleece*		
Fitzhugh	*Harriet the Spy*		
Viorst	*If I Were in Charge of the World*		
Greene	*Isabelle Shows Her Stuff*		
Manes	*It's New, It's Improved! It's Terrible!*		
Levitin	*Journey to America*		
Naidoo	*Journey to Jho'burg*		
George	*Julie of the Wolves*		
Peck	*The Life and Words of Martin Luther King Jr.*		
Smith	*Mostly Michael*		
Hoban	*Mouse and His Child*		
Cleary	*The Mouse and the Motorcycle*		
Lasky	*The Night Journey*		
Howe	*Nightly-Nightmare*		
DeClements	*Nothing's Fair in the Fifth Grade*		

NEWBERY MEDAL WINNERS

Normally appropriate for 5th - 7th graders

Gray	*Adam of the Road*	Chrisman	*Shen of the Sea*
Yates	*Amos Fortune, Free Man*	Armstrong	*Sounder*
Krumgold	*And Now Miguel*	Lenski	*Strawberry Girl*
Paterson	*Bridge to Terabithia*	Enright	*Thimble Summer*
Speare	*Bronze Bow*	Finger	*Tales From Silver Lands*
Brink	*Caddie Woodlawn*	Bois	*Twenty-One Balloons*
Sperry	*Call It Courage*	Hunt	*Up the Road Slowly*
Latham	*Carry On, Mr. Bowditch*	Armer	*Waterless Mountain*
Coatsworth	*Cat Who Went to Heaven*	Raskin	*Wasting Game*
Hawes	*Dark Frigate*	Serendy	*White Stag*
Cleary	*Dear Mr. Henshaw*	Fleischman	*Whipping Boy*
Voight	*Dicey's Song*		
Blos	*Gathering of Days*		
Mukerji	*Gay Neck: The Story of a Pigeon*		
Estes	*Ginger Pye*		
Cooper	*Grey King*		
McKinley	*Hero and the Crown*		
Alexander	*High King*		
Field	*Hitty, Her First Hundred Years*		
Fleischman	*Joyful Noise*		
Trevino	*I, Juan DePareja*		
Meigs	*Invincible Louisa*		
O'Dell	*Island of the Blue Dolphins*		
Paterson	*Jacob Have I Loved*		
Forbes	*Johnny Tremain*		
Freedman	*Lincoln: A Photobiography*		
Hamilton	*M.C. Higgins, The Great*		
Chusman	*The Midwife's Apprentice*		
Bailey	*Miss Hickory*		
O'Brien	*Mrs. Frisby and the Rats of Nimh*		
Lawson	*Rabbit Hill*		
Keith	*Rifles for Antie*		
Clark	*Secret of the Andes*		
Wojciechowska	*Shadow of a Bull*		

GRADE 6

Montgomery	*Anne of Green Gables*	Coerr	*Sadako and the Thousand Paper Cranes*
Kjelgaard	*Big Red*		
Sewell	*Black Beauty*	Avi	*S.O.R. Losers*
Sleator	*Black Briar*	Kjeigaard	*Snow Dog*
Alexander	*The Black Cauldron*	Voight	*Solitary Blue*
Lewis	*The Chronicles of Narnia*	Peck	*Soup's Goat*
Bellairs	*Curse of the Blue Figurine*	Bond	*String in the Harp*
		Babbitt	*Tuck Everlasting*
Cooper	*The Dark is Rising*	DuBois	*The Twenty-One Balloons*
Mowat	*The Dog Who Wouldn't Be*	Korman	*The War With Mr. Wizzle*
		Dejong	*Wheel on the School*
Edgdahl	*The Far Side of Evil*	Spearc	*The Witch of Blackbird Pond*
Leguin	*The Farthest Shore*		
Konigsburg	*Father's Arcane Daughter*	L'Engle	*A Wrinkle in Time*
Jukes	*Getting Even*		
Duncan	*Gift of Magic*		
McWhirter	*Guiness Book of World Records*		
Petry	*Harriet Tubman*		
King-Smith	*Harry's Mad*		
Robertson	*Henry Reed's Baby-sitting Service*		
Hurwitz	*The Hot and Cold Summer*		
Rockwell	*How to Fight a Girl*		
Uchida	*Jar of Dreams*		
Smith	*Jelly Belly*		
Forges	*Johnny Tremain*		
Collier	*Jump Ship to Freedom*		
Bellairs	*The Lamp From the Warlock's Tomb*		
Richter	*A Light in the Forest*		
Shreve	*Lucy Forever and Miss Rosetree Shrinks*		
Mott	*Master Entrick*		
Sharmat	*Mysteriously Yours Maggie Marmelstein*		
Paterson	*Park's Quest*		
Conrad	*Prairie Songs*		

SHORT STORIES

Grades 6-8

Ferber	*The Barn Cuts Off the View*
Melville	*Billy Budd*
Crane	*The Bride Comes to Yellow Sky*
Twain	*The Celebrated Jumping Frog of Calaveras County*
Benet	*The Devil and Daniel Webster*
Stockton	*The Great Stone Face*
Harte	*The Luck of Roaring Camp*
Wright	*The Man Who Saw the Flood*
Hale	*The Man Without a Country*
Poe	*The Pit and the Pendulum*
O'Henry	*The Ransom of Red Chief*
Garland	*The Return of a Private*
Irving	*Rip Van Winkle*
Stuart	*Testimony of Trees*
London	*To the Man on Trail*
Beaumont	*The Vanishing American*
Fast	*Where Are Your Guns?*
Jewett	*A White Heron*

GRADE 7

Steig	Abel's Island	Byarss	Trouble River
Rostkowski	After the Dancing Days	Reiss	The Upstairs Room
Mazer	After the Rain	Collier	War Comes to Willie Freeman
Levoy	Alan and Naomi		
Ames	Anna to the Infinite Power	Wells	War of the Worlds
		Alexander	Westmark
Fast	April Morning	Rasking	The Westing Game
Verne	Around the World in Eighty Days	LaGuin	Wizard of Earthsea
		Avi	Wolf Rider
Ullman	Banner in the Sky		
Alexander	The Beggar Queen		
Sewell	Black Beauty		
London	Call of the Wild		
Kipling	Captains Courageous		
Gilbreth	Cheaper by the Dozen		
Gunther	Death be Not Proud		
Alexander	The High King		
Tolkien	The Hobbit		
Myers	Hoops		
Doyle	The Hound of the Baskervilles		
Saroyan	The Human Comedy		
Alexande	The Illyrian Adventure		
Oneal	In Summer Light		
Irving	Legend of Sleepy Hollow		
Barrett	Lilies of the Field		
Levitin	The Mark of Conte		
Gibson	The Miracle Worker		
Howard	Mystery of the Metro		
Fox	One-Eyed Cat		
Austen	Pride and Prejudice		
Twain	The Prince and the Pauper		
Merrill	Pushcart War		
Pitts	Racing the Sun		
Lunn	The Root Cellar		
O'Dell	Sing Down the Moon		
Schaefer	Shane		
Finger	Tales From Silver Lands		
Stevenson	Treasure Island		

YOUNGER TEENS

Parents will want to help their children choose appropriate books from this list. Watch for themes that you may consider inappropriate.

Adams	*The Hitchhiker's Guide to the Galaxy*	Conklin	*P.S., I Love You; Falling in Love Again*
Auel	*Clan of the Cave Bear*	Cormier	*After the First Death; I Am the Cheese; The Chocolate War*
Bach	*The Meat in the Sandwich*		
Bates	*Love is Like Peanuts; Picking Up the Pieces*	Daly	*Seventeenth Summer*
		Dank	*Game's End*
Beagle	*The Last Unicorn*	Danziger	*Can You Sue Your Parents for Malpractice? The Cat Ate My Gymsuit; Divorce Express; The Pistachio Prescription; There's a Bat in Bunk Five*
Bennett	*The Birthday Murderer; The Dangling Witness; The Long Black Coat; The Pigeon; Say Hello to the Hitman; Then Again Maybe I Won't*		
Block	*Weetzie Bat*	Dietz	*The Jeff White Series*
Boatright	*Out of Bounds*	Duncan	*Down a Dark Hall; Chapters; Killing Mr. Griffin; Ransom; Stranger With My Face; Summer of Fear; They Never Came Home; The Third Eye*
Brady	*Please Remember Me*		
Bridgers	*Home Before Dark; Notes for Another Life*		
Brooks	*Sword of Shannara; Elfstones of Shannara; Wishsone of Shannon*		
Buchanan	*A Shining Season*	Eddings	*Pawn of Prophecy*
Clapp	*Jane Emily*	Facklam	*The Trouble with Mothers*
Cleary	*Jean and Johnny; Fifteen; The Luckiest Girl; Sister of the Bride*		
		Ferris	*Looking for Home*
		Folely	*Love by Any Other Name*
Childress	*A Hero Ain't Nothin' but a Sandwich*	Frank	*Diary of a Young Girl*
		Gallico	*The Snow Goose*
Cohen	*Phone Call From a Ghost*	George	*My Side of the Mountain*
Colman	*Accident; Boy Meets Girl; Claudia, Where Are You?*	Godfrey	*The Last War*
		Goldman	*The Princess Bride*
		Greene	*The Summer of My German Soldier*
Cooney	*Family Reunion*		
Conford	*Hail, Hail Camp Timberwood*	Hermes	*Be Still My Heart*
		Herrick	*The Perfect Guy*
		Hersey	*Hiroshima*

Hinton	*The Outsiders; Rumble Fish; Tex; That Was Then, This is Now*	O'Dell	*Hawk That Dare Not Hunt by Day*
Janeczko	*Brickyard Summer*	Sheldon	*In His Steps*
Kipling	*Captains Courageous*	Eiseley	*Immense Journey*
Lee	*To Kill a Mockingbird*	Barrett	*Lilies of the Field*
L'Engle	*Meet the Austins; The Moon by Night; A Wrinkle in Time*	Flynn	*Mister God, This Is Anna*
		Caldwell	*No One Hears but Him*
		Douglas	*The Robe*
LeGuin	*The Farthest Shore*	Berman	*The Search for Meaning*
London	*Call of the Wild; White Fang; Sea-Wolf*	Naylor	*String of Chances*
		Holmes	*Two from Galilee*
Myers	*Fat Sam, Cool Clyde, and Stuff; Hoops; Won't Know Till I Get There*	Jenkins	*Walk Across America*
		Johnson	*Wilderness Bride*
Nathan	*Portrait of Jenny*		
North	*Rascal; The Wolfling*		
Pascal	*Hanging Out With CiCi*		
Roth	*Against Incredible Odds; The Castaways; The Iceberg; Hermit; Trapped; Two for Survival*		
Twain	*Huckleberry Finn; A Connecticut Yankee in King Arthur's Court; Tom Sawyer*		
Zindel	*Pardon Me, You're Stepping on My Eyeball; The Pigman; The Pigman's Legacy; The Undertaker's Gone Bananas*		

SPIRITUAL HIGHS
Normally appropriate for teens

Lagervist	*Barabbas*
Marshall	*Beyond Ourselves*
Brancato	*Blinded by the Light*
Speare	*Bronze Bow*
Eerdman	*Eerdman's Book of Christian Poetry*
Maier	*Flames of Rome*
West	*The Friendly Persuasion*

OLDER TEENS

Books for teens often contain adult themes. We have not eliminated books here that will undoubtedly be inappropriate for some families. Parents should help their children choose from the following books.

Agee	*A Death in the Family*	Mason	*In the Country*
Allison	*Bastard Out of Carolina*	Mori	*Shizuko's Daughter*
Alvarez	*In the Time of Butterflies*	Morrison	*Beloved*
Anaya	*Bless me, Ultima*	O'Brien	*The Things They Carried: A Work of Fiction*
Angelou	*I Know Why the Caged Bird Sings*	O'Connor	*Everything That Rises Must Converge*
Bradbury	*Fahrenheit 451*		
Butler	*Parable of the Sower*	Orwell	*1984*
Card	*Ender's Game*	Potok	*The Chosen*
Chopin	*The Awakening*	Power	*The Grass Dancer*
Cisneros	*The House on Mango Street*	Salinger	*The Catcher in the Rye*
		Shaara	*Killer Angels*
Ellison	*The Invisible Man*	Steinbeck	*The Grapes of Wrath*
Emecheta	*Bride Price*	Uchida	*Picture Bride*
Faulkner	*The Bear*	Watson	*Montana 1948*
Frazier	*Cold Mountain*	Wright	*Native Son*
Gaines	*A Lesson Before Dying*	Yolen	*Briar Rose*
Gardner	*Grendel*		
Gibbons	*Ellen Foster*		
Golding	*Lord of the Flies*		
Heller	*Catch-22*		
Hemingway	*A Farewell to Arms*		
Hesse	*Siddhartha*		
Huxley	*Brave New World*		
Keneally	*Schindler's List*		
King	*The Beekeeper's Apprentice, or on the Segregation of the Queen*		
Kosinski	*Painted Bird*		
Lee	*To Kill a Mockingbird*		
LeGuin	*The Left Hand of Darkness*		
McCullers	*The Member of the Wedding*		
McKinley	*Beauty*		
Malamud	*The Fixer*		
Markandaya	*Nectar in a Sieve*		

GREAT CLASSICS

Normally appropriate for Teens (and Adults)

The following listing consists of what are considered the greatest writings of Western minds. These pieces take considerable reading skill and much thought. Truly educated adults have an acquaintance with these writers and their works. When your children are juniors and seniors in high school they should be introduced to many of these great thinkers.

Homer (about 9th century)	*Illiad, Odyssey*
The Old Testament	
Aeschylus (about 500-450 B.C.)	Tragedies
Herodotus (480-425 B.C.)	(Persian Wars)
Euripides (480-425 B.C.)	Tragedies
Thucydides (460-400 B.C.)	*History of the Peloponnesian War*
Hippocrates (460-370 B.C.)	Medical writing
Aristophanes (450-380 B.C.)	Comedies: *The Clouds, The Birds, The Frogs*
Plato (428-347 B.C.)	*The Republic, Symposium, Sophist, Phaedrus*
Aristotle (380-320 B.C.)	*Poetics, Ethics, Politics*
Virgil (75-20 B.C.)	Works
Horace (65-7 B.C.)	Works
Livy (60-7 B.C.)	*History of Rome*
Ovid (45 B.C.-A.D. 20)	*Metamorphosis*
Plutarch (45-120)	*Lives of the Noble Grecians and Romans*
Marcus Aurelius (120-180)	*Meditations*
The New Testament	
St. Augustine (350-430)	*Confessions, The City of God, On Christian Doctrine*
St. Thomas Aquinas (1225-1275)	*Summa Theologica*
Dante (1265-1320)	*The Divine Comedy*
Goeffrey Chaucer (1340-1400)	*Canterbury Tales*
Leonardo da Vinci (1450-1520)	*Notebooks*
Machiavelli (1470-1525)	*The Prince*
Sir Thomas More (1480-1535)	*Utopia*
Martin Luther (1480-1545)	*Three Treatises*
John Calvin (1500-1565)	*Institutes of the Christian Religion*
Miguel de Cervantes (1547-1616)	*Don Quixote*
Francis Bacon (1560-1625)	*Advancement of Learning*
William Shakespeare (1565-1616)	Works
Thomas Hobbes (1588-1679)	*The Leviathan*
Descartes (1595-1650)	*Rules for the Direction of the Mind*
John Milton (1622-1673)	*Paradise Lost*

Moliere	*The Miser, The School for Wives, The Misanthrope, Tartuffe*
Benedict de Spinoza (1630-1675)	*Ethics*
John Locke (1632-1704)	*Letter Concerning Toleration, Thoughts Concerning Education*
Daniel Defoe (1660-1730)	*Robinson Crusoe*
Jonathan Swift 1667-1745)	*Gulliver's Travels, A Modest Proposal*
Alexander Pope (1688-1745)	*Rape of the Lock, Essay on Man*
Voltaire (1694-1778)	*Candide*
Henry Fielding (1707-1784)	*Tom Jones*
Samuel Johnson (1709-1785)	*The Lives of the Poets*
David Hume (1711-1776)	*Treatise of Human Nature, An Inquiry Concerning Human Understanding*
Jean-Jacques Rousseau (1712-1778)	*The Social Contract*
Laurence Sterne (1713-1767)	*Tristram Shandy*
Immanuel Kant (1729-1804)	*Critique of Pure Reason, Critique of Practical Reason*
Edward Gibbon (1737-1795)	*The Decline and Fall of the Roman Empire*
James Boswell (1740-1795)	*London Journal, Life of Samuel Johnson*
John Jay, James Madison, Alexander Hamilton (1745-1836)	*Federalist Papers, Declaration of Independence*
Johann Wolfgang von Goethe (1749-1832)	*Faust*
George Wilhelm Fredrich Hegel (1770-1850)	*Philosophy of Right*
William Wordsworth (1970-1850)	Poems
Samuel Taylor Coleridge (1772-1834)	Poems
Jane Austen (1775-1817)	*Pride and Prejudice*
Ralph Waldo Emerson (1803-1882)	Essays
Nathaniel Hawthorne (1804-1864)	*The Scarlet Letter*
Alexis de Tocqueville (1805-1859)	*Democracy in America*
John Stuart Mill (1805-1873)	*On Liberty, Utilitarianism*
Charles Darwin (1809-1882)	*The Origin of Species, The Descent of Man*
Charles Dickens (1812-1878)	*David Copperfield*
Henry David Thoreau (1817-1862)	*Walden, Civil Disobedience*
George Eliot (1819-1891)	*Middlemarch*
Herman Melville (1819-1890)	*Moby Dick*
Fyodor Dostoevsky (1821-1881)	*Crime and Punishment, The Brothers Karamazov*
Gustave Flaubert (1821-1880)	*Madame Bovary*
Henrik Ibsen (1828-1906)	Plays: *Hedda Gabler, A Doll's House*
Leo Tolstoy (1828-1910)	*War and Peace*
Mark Twain (1835-1910)	*The Adventures of Huckleberry Finn, The Mysterious Stranger*
Henry James (1843-1916)	*The Ambassadors*
Sigmund Freud (1856-1939)	*The Interpretation of Dreams*

George Bernard Shaw (1856-1950)	*Man and Superman, Saint Joan, Pygmalion*
John Dewey (1859-1952)	*Democracy and Education*
Alfred North Whitehead (1861-1947)	*The Aims of Education and Other Essays, Adventures of Ideas*
Marcel Proust (1871-1922)	*Remembrance of Things Past*
Bertrand Russell (1872-1970)	*An Inquiry into Meaning and Truth*
Thomas Mann (1875-1955)	*The Magic Mountain*
James Joyce (1882-1941)	*Portrait of the Artist as a Young Man*
Albert Einstein (1879-1955)	*The Meaning of Relativity*
Franz Kafka (1883-1924)	*The Trial*
Arnold Toynbee (1889-1983)	*A Study of History*
Jean Paul Sartre (1905-1975)	*Being and Nothingness*
Aleksandr I Solzhenitsyn (1918-)	*Cancer Ward*

INDEX

Order Form

To place your *Writing Strands* order, simply fill out this form and send it to us by mail or by fax. If you would like to get your order started even faster, go to the *Writing Strands* website and place your order online at: www.writingstrands.com

		QTY	Total
Writing Strands 1 Oral Work for ages 3-8	$14.95 ea.	___	_____
Writing Strands 2 About 7 years old	$18.95 ea.	___	_____
Writing Strands 3 Starting program ages 8-12	$18.95 ea.	___	_____
Writing Strands 4 Any age after Level 3 or starting program at age 13 or 14	$18.95 ea.	___	_____
Writing Strands 5 Any age after Level 4 or starting program at age 15 or 16	$20.95 ea.	___	_____
Writing Strands 6 17 or any age after Level 5	$20.95 ea.	___	_____
Writing Strands 7 18 or any age after Level 6	$22.95 ea.	___	_____
Writing Exposition Senior high school and after Level 7	$22.95 ea.	___	_____
Creating Fiction Senior high school and after Level 7	$22.95 ea.	___	_____
Evaluating Writing Parents' manual for all levels of *Writing Strands*	$19.95 ea.	___	_____
Reading Strands Parents' manual for story and book interpretation, all grades	$22.95 ea.	___	_____
Communication and Interpersonal Relationships Communication Manners (teens)	$17.95 ea.	___	_____
Basic Starter Set (SAVE $5.00) *Writing Strands 2, Writing Strands 3, Reading Strands* and *Evaluating Writing*	$75.80 per set	___	_____
Intermediate Starter Set (SAVE $10.00) *Writing Strands 3, Writing Strands 4, Evaluating Writing, Communication and Interpersonal Relationships* and *Reading Strands*	$88.75 per set	___	_____
Advanced Starter Set (SAVE $30.00) *Writing Strands 5, Writing Strands 6, Writing Strands 7, Writing Exposition, Creating Fiction, Evaluating Writing, Communication and Interpersonal Relationships* and *Reading Strands*	$138.60 per set	___	_____
Dragonslaying Is for Dreamers – Package 1st novel in *Dragonslaying* trilogy (Early teens) and parents' manual for analyzing the novel.	$18.95 ea.	___	_____
Dragonslaying Is for Dreamers Novel only	$9.95 ea.	___	_____
Axel Meets the Blue Men 2nd novel in *Dragonslaying* trilogy (Teens)	$9.95 ea.	___	_____
Axel's Challenge Final novel in *Dragonslaying* trilogy (Teens)	$9.95 ea.	___	_____
Dragonslaying Trilogy All three novels in series	$25.00 set	___	_____
Dragonslaying Trilogy and Parents' Manual Three novels plus parents' manual for first novel	$32.99 set	___	_____

SUBTOTAL (use this total to calculate shipping) _____

Texas residents: Add 8.25% sales tax _____

U.S. Shipping: $6 for orders up to $75 _____

$8 for orders over $75 _____

Outside U.S. Shipping: $4 per book. **$12 minimum.** _____

TOTAL U.S. FUNDS _____

Mail your check or money order or fill in your credit card information below:

◯ VISA   ◯ Discover   ◯ Master Card

Account Number _____

Expiration date: Month _____ Year _____

Signature **X** _____

We ship UPS to the 48 states, so please no P.O. Box addresses. PLEASE PRINT

Name _____

Street _____

City _____ State ____ Zip _____

Phone (_____) _____

Email _____

SHIPPING INFORMATION

CONTINENTAL U.S.: We ship via UPS ground service. Most customers will receive their orders within 10 business days.

ALASKA, HAWAII, U.S. MILITARY ADDRESSES AND US TERRITORIES: We ship via U.S. Priority Mail. Orders generally arrive within 2 weeks.

OUTSIDE U.S.: We generally ship via Air Mail. Delivery times vary.

RETURNS

Our books are guaranteed to please you. If they do not, return them within 30 days and we'll refund the full purchase price.

PRIVACY

We respect your privacy. We will not sell, rent or trade your personal information.

INQUIRIES AND ORDERS

Phone:	(800) 688-5375
Fax:	(888) 663-7855 TOLL FREE
Write:	*Writing Strands* 624 W. University, Suite 248T Denton, TX 76201-1889
E-mail:	info@writingstrands.com
Website:	www.writingstrands.com

Writing Strands

TO ORDER EVEN FASTER, GO ONLINE AT:

www.writingstrands.com

Prices valid through 03/31/06